BEDSIDE BOOK
OF
MURDER

CONTENTS

1

THE BURNING BODY

At about 4 o'clock on a Sunday morning in 1876, a certain Mrs Scrivener was woken from her sleep by a loud noise. Sitting bolt upright in bed, she strained her ears to hear what it was and where it came from. But all was now silent. The lady waited a few moments to reassure herself that the noise would not repeat itself, then snuggled down again under the warmth of her heavy blankets. But just as her head had found a nice warm groove among the pillows the boom of a heavy object falling to the floor echoed through the wall. Evidently something untoward was going on in the house next door. Mrs Scrivener was wide awake now, and there was little chance of her getting back to sleep.

Around the same time Thomas Whitely, a lamplighter who worked for the Leighton Buzzard Gas Company, was walking his familiar ro ute in the streets outside. In the quiet of the night he was startled by a scream. He stood stock still, hardly daring to breathe. After a few seconds he heard the cry "Murder!" and then, once again, all was silent.

Somewhere at the end of the row of houses, the disappearing form of a cat or a fox caught the lamplighter's eye. He sighed with relief. Perhaps he hadn't heard anything after all. In the dead of night, when there is nobody to talk to, it is easy to let your imagination run away with you. Thomas Whitely walked on, going about his work.

Shortly after 5 o'clock that same morning, Charles

Greeves, a flagman working for the Great Western Railways, was on his way home. He was used to the night shift, but he still welcomed the thought of a hot mug of tea and a warm bed. As he walked up the street of terraced houses in the pre-dawn gloom, trying not to make too much noise with his boots, he was startled by the figure of a woman sitting on her doorstep. She was crying and her head was covered by a large, red shawl. As Greeves approached she looked up, making no attempt to disguise her tears. He tried to coax her troubles out of her, but she refused to speak. She merely continued sobbing. The flagman was in no mood to hang around. It was cold, it was late and he wanted to get home. Soon enough he had taken his leave of the woman and had walked away.

Little did these three individuals know that what they had witnessed and heard that night was one of the most macabre and mysterious deaths in British legal history.

On October 15th, 1876, in the house next door to Mrs Scrivener's, Mary Ann Favel, a 26-year-old woman, was undergoing an extraordinarily gruesome and agonizing demise. Her head was being beaten and her body covered with benzoline. She was then set alight.

In the morning, when her corpse was discovered, Mary Ann's flesh was so badly charred that, when touched, it fell away from her bones like meat that had been overcooked. The cinders that were once her clothes lay in ashes all around her. Nothing about her was recognisable anymore. Nothing, that is, save for a few coins she still clutched in her right fist. They came to a total of tenpence ha'penny.

No fewer than seven people had been sleeping at the Favel house that night. But, if they were to be believed, not one of them had been roused by any disturbance. All professed utter ignorance of Mary Ann's fate until Jane Favel, the 51-year-old widowed matriarch of the family, discovered her daughter's frizzled corpse on the kitchen floor just before breakfast time.

Police were not slow to suggest that at least one of them had to be lying. With no sign of a break-in nor any evidence of a fight, it seemed that no other explanation was possible. Thus, despite all their protestations of horror and outrage, three members of the Favel clan, including Mary Ann's mother, were duly arrested and taken into custody.

The suspects spent a long time at the police station, repeating their stories and accounting for their movements. Again and again they were asked to relate exactly what had happened on the fatal night and, each time, they diligently repeated their accounts. Not once did their stories change. All of them insisted that they had slept the night soundly and nothing unusual had happened. Eventually the police had to admit defeat. All three Favels returned home.

In the meantime news of the murder had hit the headlines. The case was reported in all its gory detail, horrifying people throughout Bedfordshire and the surrounding areas. Nothing like it had happened before and, once the police admitted that they had yet to catch the villain, cries for action became loud and strong. ·

Something had to be done and, eventually, a reward of £100 was offered up for information that would lead to an arrest. It was a vast sum of money for the time, but it was a necessary expense to quell the public's unrest. And it certainly brought a quick response.

Isaac Favel was the first to come to the police station and point the finger of suspicion at Mary Ann's mother. Then Mrs White, a vague acquaintance of Jane Favel's, came forward with some scraps of overheard gossip which she also thought proved the woman's guilt. Finally, a Mrs Chandler approached the police with what seemed to be the most damning testimony of all - a confession from the killer.

"It was the day the police let her go," the elderly lady explained, "Jane Favel came to my house and we had a drink of warm beer. Then she and I walked down the street together." According to Mrs Chandler it was then Jane Favel made her confession. "She would not give me tenpence ha'penny," she told her old friend, "so I hit her over the head with a stick and then I poured oil over her."

Chandler went on to say that, with the killing done, Jane Favel was overcome with remorse. "I couldn't stop in the house after what I'd done," she had confessed, "I went out and sat on the doorstep."

Mrs Chandler's account tied in neatly with the evidence of Charles Greeves. It seemed to make sense. Mrs Jane Favel was thus rearrested and charged with the murder of her daughter. However, as the trial date approached and no harder evidence emerged, the police knew that they were clutching at straws.

Jane Favel's defence counsel was no genius, but he had little difficulty in discrediting the vast majority of witnesses who appeared in the dock. Their testimony, he pointed out, was almost entirely hearsay, most of it picked up from the daily papers. And, of Mrs Chandler, he was particularly scathing. Turning to the jury he sneered: "Would you entrust your confession to a seventy-year-old lady who is practically deaf?"

A densely packed courtroom listened in silence to the only verdict that the jury could really deliver. Jane Favel was declared not guilty.

Jane Favel was released without a stain on her character and walked from the court a free woman.

Mary Ann Favel was burned to death in a house in which her mother and six other people slept. Not one of them, it seems, was awakened by her screams or by the stench of her burning flesh. She died clutching tenpence ha'penny in her fist and nobody, to this day, knows why.

2

THE WIFE, THE REVEREND
AND THE CHLOROFORM

Thomas Edward Bartlett, a prosperous London grocer, had a curious view of marriage. He believed that a man should have two wives, one for companionship and one, as he put it, "for use." When he met sixteen-year-old Adelaide Blanche de la Tremoille he put her firmly in the former category and thus, following their marriage in 1875, he didn't take her to his bed. Instead he dispatched her to a boarding-school for two years and thence to a covent in Belgium for twelve months.

This attractive French girl was somewhat bemused by the arrangement but she accepted it in good heart. Indeed when, refined and cultivated, she was finally permitted to return to London, she and Thomas enjoyed a number of years of comparative bliss. And yet all was not well. Whilst Thomas loved talking to his wife and was hugely entertained by her conversation, he still insisted that, as far as sex was concerned, he preferred to be serviced elsewhere. Prostitutes and casual lovers attended to his animal needs whilst poor Adelaide had to be satisfied with her books. Eventually, and not too surprisingly, she declared that this was unendurable.

As luck would have it, however, it was around this time that this unusual couple came across the Reverend George Dyson, an engaging young minister of the local Methodist Chapel and a man destined to alleviate Adelaide's frustrations. The three met at a Sunday service in the autumn of 1885 and liked each other immediately. It was quickly agreed that Dyson should become a regular visitor to the Bartlett home. Thomas suggested that he would even be able to pay Dyson for his trouble if he would consent to giving his wife some extra instruction in mathematics, Latin and history. Dyson readily agreed.

It was not long, of course, before the relationship between Adelaide and the Reverend grew to be more than just friendship. The hours that they spent together soon spawned a tender intimacy that was clear for all to see. Thomas Bartlett noticed it too. And yet, whilst most husbands would have found this unbearable, he found it enchanting. Dyson, he thought, would make an excellent lover for his wife and he actively encouraged their blossoming romance. It delighted him that the couple should kiss in his presence, go for long walks together in public and spend long hours together in private. When Dyson wrote Adelaide love letters Thomas even wrote back to thank him.

In December 1885, Thomas Bartlett was taken ill. Adelaide summoned the local physician, a Dr Leach, who made an initial examination. The doctor found the patient to be suffering from nausea, diarrhoea and haemorrhage of the bowels, he also remarked on how Thomas appeared tired and depressed. But he was unable to give a specific diagnosis for these ills. Dr Dudley, another physician and a colleague of Dr Leach was summoned for a second opinion. His examination revealed little more, but at least he had a conclusion to draw. Dr Dudley suggested that Thomas Bartlett was, essentially, in perfectly good health but suffering from some kind of hysteria. He recommended rest and care. That, he said, was probably all that was needed.

Adelaide responded to this recommendation with alacrity. She had a bed placed in the drawing room for her husband to use and nursed him with the utmost devotion. She stayed by his bedside day and night, sleeping in a chair next to him and cradling his foot in her hand, an action

Thomas said he found comforting. She cooked his food and served his meals, mopped his brow and brushed his hair. Hardly a moment went by when she wasn't catering to his needs and looking after his well being. As a result Thomas made steady, if not spectacular, progress.

On December 26th George Dyson called at the house, anxious to see how the patient was faring. He had grown very fond of Thomas Bartlett, regarding him almost as a brother, and had been most distressed by his recent illness. The two men spent the afternoon together and Dyson was delighted to find Thomas so much improved and in such thoroughly good spirits. Before he left, however, Adelaide warned him that things were not as good as they seemed. Thomas was still suffering from an "internal complaint" which was giving him considerable pain. She mentioned that she needed to obtain some chloroform to soothe him and help him sleep. She needed quite a large quantity.

The following day, Dyson called at three chemist's shops, obtaining small bottles of chloroform at each. He told the staff at each shop that he needed the chloroform to remove grease-spots from clothes. He later transferred the contents of the three small bottles to a larger bottle and this he handed to Adelaide the following day during a stroll by the river at Putney.

In the meantime Thomas Bartlett's health continued to make good progress. Indeed, by the following Tuesday, New Year's Eve, he seemed to have recovered entirely. He spent the morning with Dr Leach at his dentist's and the afternoon in the company of a few friends at his home. It was a small gathering, but a lively one. Ready to greet the New Year, Thomas was eagerly talking about the future and his plans for a brief winter holiday in Torquay.

His appetite had returned too. He ate and drank heartily during the party and then, for supper, he devoured oysters, cake and tea. Before retiring to bed at about 10 o'clock he gave the maid his order for breakfast. He said he would like a large haddock.

The maid brought in coals for the night at about 10.30.

When she left, Adelaide came out of the sick-room with her and told her to leave a basin for the master's beef-tea on the table in the landing. Adelaide Bartlett then returned, as usual, to be by her husband's bedside.

At 4 a.m. the following morning, Adelaide came out of the drawing room looking pale and shaken. She woke the maid and ordered her to fetch Dr Leach immediately. "I think that Thomas is dead," she cried.

Dr Leach arrived thirty minutes later, astounded to find a man who had been in perfect health the previous day lying lifeless across the bed. He immediately suspected that Thomas had taken poison, but Adelaide declared it would have been impossible for him to have done so without her noticing. The doctor searched the room, but found nothing suspicious. He then told Adelaide that there would have to be a post mortem.

Two doctors from the Charing Cross Hospital were called in to perform the examination. They found no natural cause of death but the stomach contents gave rise to suspicion and they ordered further tests. Bartlett's stomach was later found to contain a large quantity of chloroform.

Inevitably, Adelaide Bartlett was arrested and charged with the murder of her husband. George Dyson was arrested also, for being an accessory before the fact.

The case aroused great national interest by the time the trial opened on Monday, April 12th, 1886, at the Old Bailey. There was a sensation when the Crown decided to offer no evidence against George Dyson and the judge formally asked the jury to declare him "not guilty." But the charge against Adelaide Bartlett was still left to be proved.

As she stood alone in the dock, where so many murderers had been sentenced to death before, the public gazed at her with a morbid curiosity. Was this attractive French woman to hang by her neck from a coarse hempen rope?

The answer was "No." The prosecution opened full of hope and confidence, but their case rapidly deteriorated. Chloroform is a strong poison and was undeniably the cause of Thomas Bartlett's death, but how it got from the bottle into his stomach was a question that no one seemed able to answer. Liquid chloroform being extremely caustic, it would have burnt his throat and mouth. But the autopsy revealed no signs of inflammation in these areas, or else-where, where the poison would have also been expected to burn. Moreover, having such a chemical poured into his mouth, Bartlett should have screamed and groaned. But no one heard any noises that night. There was a great deal of circumstantial evidence to point to Adelaide's guilt, but few facts to support it.

The trial did reveal that Adelaide had not acquired the chloroform to ease her husband's pain. She had used it instead to dampen his ardour. It also revealed the bizarre facts of the Bartletts' marriage and her strange liaison with the Reverend Dyson. The prosecution made much of the contraceptives that had been found in Thomas Bartlett's coat and the sex manual that had been found at his home. But these things, whilst providing great entertainment for the court, seemed scarcely relevant to the matter of murder.

In the face of a brilliant defence by Sir Edward Clarke, the prosecution finally wilted. "You are asked to believe," he announced, "that a woman who had for years lived in friendship and affection with her husband, who had nursed him and tended him night and day, who had called in doctors and tried to cheer him up, had suddenly been transformed into a murderess, committing a crime, not only without excuse, but absolutely without any object, by the execution of a delicate operation difficult for the highest trained doctors to perform. This is the first case in the world in which it has been suggested that a person was murdered by the administration of liquid chloroform. There is no other case of the kind - and yet it is now suggested to you that Adelaide Bartlett has committed an offence absolutely unknown in the history of medical jurisprudence."

The Old Bailey jury retired at 4.10 p.m. and returned 50 minutes later with a verdict of not guilty.

But they did add this rider: "Although we think grave

suspicion is attached to the prisoner, we do not think there is sufficient evidence to show how or by whom the chloroform was administered to the deceased."

After the trial, Sir James Paget, the noted surgeon, is said to have remarked: "Mrs Bartlett was no doubt properly acquitted. Now she should tell us, in the interests of medical science, how she did it."

Adelaide Bartlett, however, never did tell.

3

THE HORROR OF THE STAUNTONS

At 34, Harriet presented the picture of a healthy young woman. Unfortunately, however, all was not quite as it seemed. The poor girl was mentally retarded. Harriet had never been able to read and write, although her private tutors had been patient and persevering. Moreover, she had spells of sudden obduracy which, as her family had learnt, often led to violent temper tantrums. She was, in short, a very difficult lady to deal with.

In 1874, to give her parents a welcome break, Harriet went to live with an aunt in Walworth, south-east London. It was here where her fortunes seemed to change. Previously she had always been shunned by the neighbours and certainly no menfolk would give her the time of day. But, all of a sudden, Harriet found herself a beau. He was a young man of 24, an auctioneer's clerk who went by the name of Louis Staunton.

Staunton had rather obvious good looks and Harriet clearly found him enchanting. It was a huge novelty to be escorted about town by a man, especially someone ten years her junior, and Harriet lapped it up. They spent a good deal of time together. Harriet swooned at all the compliments he showered on her and delighted in all the stories he would tell. Never once did she suspect that his motives where anything other than pure.

Louis Staunton, however, was not the man he made

himself out to be. It was not Harriet's charms that had attracted him, it was her private fortune. This amounted to very nearly £4,000.

Staunton was no lawyer, but he knew that should a woman marry with no legally drawn-up marriage settlement, her possessions on marriage passed automatically to her husband. It was with this in mind that he began his seduction. And, already, he could see that it was working.

Harriet's mother was quick to spot the danger. She had lived for years with the fear of her feeble-witted daughter marrying someone intent on getting his hands on her money and now those fears were turning into fact. Harriet was of course blind to the protests. She simply refused to listen. But her mother persisted. She had no doubts what Louis Staunton had in mind. Finally, she resorted to the cruellest weapon of all. She made an application to the Court of Chancery for her daughter, bluntly described as a lunatic, to become its ward.

Alas, this application did not succeed. What it did do, however, was to convince Harriet that she could no longer trust her own family. Her future happiness, she decided, now lay in the hands of strangers. Her engagement to Louis Staunton was announced.

Harriet was quickly introduced to Staunton's relatives including his half-brother Patrick and Patrick's wife, Elizabeth. She also met Elizabeth's sister, Alice Rhodes. These individuals were now her new family and the most significant people in her life. Indeed, when she married Louis in Clapham Church on a June day in 1875 it was only these three, besides the bride and groom and the officiating clergyman, who were present.

Once married, the newly-weds set up home in a house in Loughborough Park Road, Brixton. Little is known of what went on in those early days, but one doubts if it was good. Harriet's mother came to see her once and thought that her daughter seemed pale. But it was a brief visit. Ten minutes was all that Staunton allowed before rudely directing his new mother-in-law back on to the street outside.

The woman returned to the house sometime later, when, by chance, Louis was not there and was able to stay a little longer. But even then she clearly wasn't wanted. Once Staunton had heard about her visit, he made sure she would not make the trip again. Putting pen to paper he wrote a letter that left no scope for doubt:

"I hear from my sister that you called and wished to see your daughter. I only wish I had been there at the time. Now, I tell you once and for all, after your unnatural and brutal conduct to her, she never wishes to see you again nor would I allow her to do so. In fact, while you live, she considers she is in danger for her life."

Louis Staunton must have smirked as he wrote this piece of vitriol. He knew all too well that the danger to Harriet's life came not from her mother but from himself. But, even though he had already begun to hasten her demise, his hapless wife was not yet aware of her fate.

Soon after their marriage, Alice Rhodes moved in with the Stauntons and became the mistress of Harriet's new husband. Harriet protested, of course, but already she was too weak to do so effectively. Her food was already being rationed. She was also too weak to carry a child, though carry a child she did. In March 1876 Harriet Staunton gave birth to a baby boy.

Childbirth is cause for rejoicing in most households, but not at the Staunton's home. Louis never looked at his child nor even bothered to give him a name. The boy was just an inconvenience. Barely three months had passed before Louis decided that the infant must leave. He also decided that Harriet should go too.

The mother and son were thus dispatched to the country to live with Louis's brother, Patrick Staunton, his wife and their two children at The Woodlands, Cudham in Kent. Patrick did not object to the arrangement, for he profited handsomely from the deal. But if anyone expected that he would take care of mother and child, they would have been sorely mistaken.

Harriet lived day and night in the back bedroom of the

small five-roomed house where she slept on a piece of board laid across three trestles. Her child, during its wretched life, slept beside her in a bassinette covered only with a shawl. In October 1876 Harriet was allowed out for the first time. But only to go up to London to sign some papers that gave over the rest of her fortune to her husband. When that was done she was returned to Cudham and to her squalid prison without a moment's notice.

It was a wonder that she and her boy survived as long as they did. But, by the beginning of 1877, it was clear that they could not last much longer. The child lingered until April, before dying of inanition, or exhaustion from want of food. His mother tarried a while more. But death was now inevitable.

Harriet Staunton had been systematically starved for months. She was now just skin and bone with barely enough strength to stand. She had not been allowed to wash and, as a consequence, her body was filthy and swarming with vermin. Her head was alive with lice, her body was covered in sores. Even the heartless Louis felt a shiver of pity as he gazed at her pathetic form.

Louis Stanton had foreseen that, if his wife died at Cudham, awkward questions might be asked. So, on April 12th he and and his sister-in-law booked accommodation for an "invalid lady" at a house in Penge, London. Then they returned to The Woodlands and half-carried, half-dragged poor Harriet to a wagon that would take them to the station at Bromley where, being too weak to stand, whe was lifted into the train. When they arrived at Penge she was lifted out again and, amidst groans and sobs, was placed in a chair. Elizabeth Staunton tried to pacify her with the promise of food. "All right," she said, "You will have your supper directly." It quietened her a little.

Two men assisted Harriet into a cab and she was driven to 34 Forbes Road where Louis Staunton had engaged the rooms for the "invalid." She was taken upstairs and put into bed.

By now it was clear to everyone that it was too late for

Harriet to recover and, for the first time, they sent for a doctor. The next day Dr Dean Longrigg came and was told lie upon lie about epilepsy and other fictitious ailments. He immediately saw that there was nothing he could do and waited patiently until just after 11 o'clock, when Harriet Staunton died.

Dr Longrigg had no reason to doubt the Stauntons' statements and certified that Harriet had died from cerebral disease and apoplexy. The following day, however, he had second thoughts. He withdrew the certificate and communicated with the coroner.

A post-mortem examination was carried out on April 19th, 1877, and its findings made it clear that Harriet's death had not been a natural one. Her body weight, a mere five stone four pounds, was roughly half what it should have been. There was not a particle of fat upon her body.

The police lost no time in taking their cue from the coroner's report. The Staunton brothers and their women-folk were arrested and lodged in Maidstone Gaol. On September 19th, 1877, all four appeared at the Old Bailey to face charges of murder. All four were found guilty and sentenced to death.

It was shortly after the trial that the respected medical journal, The Lancet, decided to query the findings. It commented that before murder by starvation could be proved it was necessary to prove death by starvation. The post-mortem, they declared, did not provide a convincing argument that death had occured this way. Tuberculosis could have been the culprit, as could many other diseases.

As a consequence of this report, the Home Secretary felt compelled to re-examine the case. Two days before the death sentences were carried out, all four were saved, their punishments commuted to imprisonment.

The decision was received with mixed feelings by the public. A fortnight later, when Alice Rhodes was granted a free pardon, the news caused no great sensation.

The three Stauntons served lifetime prison sentences, but only one of them, Patrick, died in prison. His wife was released quietly after four years and disappeared, grateful for the chance to forget a dreadful past. Louis, who had gained most from the brutal treatment of his wife, was given his liberty some years later. He too disappeared into obscurity.

But though the villains escaped with their lives, their crime was not forgotten. Five years later, as a direct consequence of the Staunton case, the Married Women's Property Act became law. Henceforth, a woman who married retained all her rights in her own property. She was no longer a mere chattel of the man she married. Harriet Staunton had thus not died in vain.

4

MURDER AMONG THE RULING CLASSES

If ever a man was bound to be murdered it was Josslyn Hay, Earl of Erroll. A large slice of the white male population of the pre-war African colony of Kenya wanted him dead. And so did some of the women — particularly the unattractive ones.

Rich, and handsome with it, Erroll had one overriding philosophy: women, particularly if they were beautiful and married, were there to be seduced, and their husbands to be blatantly cuckolded.

Erroll was already a notorious philanderer before he arrived in East Africa in the mid1920s but, once there, and married to Idina de la Warr, a woman with a reputation almost as bad as his, his exploits became legendary. "Clouds," the couples' luxury home in the White Highlands of Kenya, became known as the centre of "Happy Valley" and its reputation for infidelity and waywardness was soon the talk of the empire.

Idina probably gave wife-swapping its first boost in civilised society. All her guest bedrooms had duplicate keys which were laid out on a hall table. Thus, partners could be chosen at will, or by bizarre games of chance. Night and day, bedroom doors were opened and closed with heaves and sighs echoing all around.

Alcohol was prevalent too, as were the new drugs of the age. The champagne-swilling Happy Valley set would inject themselves with morphine without a second thought and took cocaine as liberally as snuff.

Erroll and Idina revelled in all this decadence. And yet there were limits. Whilst Idina tolerated, even encouraged, Erroll's casual affairs a permanent mistress was another matter. When Erroll found one in the shape of Molly Ramsay-Hill, the young wife of a wealthy cattle-rancher, Idina quickly filed for divorce. This was readily granted, and Erroll married Molly in 1930.

Their marriage was not a success. Molly had hoped to reform her husband and, once she realised there was no hope of this dream coming true, she turned more and more to drink and drugs for solace. He, in turn, told the servants to give her all she wanted. "If she wants to die, let her have it," he ordered. Terrified of their master, the servants obeyed. Molly died in 1939, a hopeless alcoholic and drug addict.

It was a tragedy, of course. But it did little to dampen the joy of Happy Valley. Life there continued much as before, the night-and-day parties scandalising both white and black communities through their extravagance.

At the end of 1940 another aristocratic misfit arrived from Britain to join in the hedonistic lifestyle of the 39-year-old Erroll. He was Sir Jock Delves Broughton, a wealthy landowner from Cheshire. Broughton had just married an attractive, blonde, blue-eyed beauty called Diana Caldwell. At 27, she was half her husband's age and was easy prey for the philandering Erroll.

Within the week, Diana and Erroll had begun an affair and were boldly declaring their passion to the world. An old friend, Commander Jack Soames, wisely advised Broughton to cut his losses and leave Kenya straight away. But Broughton refused to listen. Instead he chose to confront the lovers.

Diana readily admitted the affair, as did Erroll. But neither of them agreed to call it off. In fact, Erroll insisted that he would go on seeing Broughton's wife for as long as he pleased. Broughton was enraged but powerless.

On January 23rd, 1941, it seemed that Broughton had accepted his role as the loser. He organised a dinner party for Erroll, Diana and a family friend, Mrs June Carberry, at the Muthaiga Country Club.

Suddenly, champagne glass in hand, he rose to propose a toast to his wife and her seducer. "I wish them every happiness, and may their union be blessed with an heir!" he boomed.

Broughton left for his home soon afterwards, taking Mrs Carberry with him. He left his wife in the company of Erroll, merely telling him to return Diana home no later than 3.00 a.m.

As it turned out, the couple returned earlier than expected, at 2.30 a.m. and, after talking for a while downstairs, Diana retired to her own bedroom and Erroll drove off into the rainy night.

At 3.30 a.m., Broughton knocked on Mrs Carberry's door, asking whether she needed anything. She declined his offer sleepily and he went away, ostensibly back to his own room.

Five hours later, two African dairyworkers, plodding along the highway eight miles outside Nairobi, saw the headlights of a stationary car blazing through the pre- dawn drizzle. They went up to investigate and found Erroll slumped, dog-like on all fours, beneath the steering-wheel. A bullet had been shot through his head, another was lodged in the floor nearby.

Broughton was the obvious suspect, although he insisted that he had been at home all night. He was prepared to call Mrs Carberry to testify about his 3.30 a.m. knock, but the police arrested him for murder all the same.

In due course, Sir Jock Delves Broughton was brought to trial where the evidence against him was substantial. But it was not enough to convict. Helped by a sensational defence by one of South Africa's most brilliant advocates, Broughton was acquitted and left the court a free man.

Despite the verdict, Broughton was discreetly condemned by Kenyan white society, which, by then, had tired of the self-indulgent goings-on in Happy Valley while faraway Britain was on her knees and fighting to ward off a German invasion. He was reunited with Diana, but all social doors were firmly closed. A year later, depressed and partly paralysed from a fall, Broughton committed suicide with an overdose of drugs in Liverpool's Adelphi Hotel.

He left a note, but it was only a rambling account of the Erroll incident. It was certainly no confession of murder. Nonetheless, as Diana Broughton would declare many years later: "No, he never admitted that he did it... but he never denied it either."

The intriguing question, of course, is if he was guilty how did he do it?

The only likely explanation is that Broughton hid in the back of Erroll's car before it left his home that night. When it reached that lonely stretch of road, he got up and shot the peer in the head. Then he ditched the car in the gravel-pit and ran back home - as a big-game hunter he was fit enough to do that - waking Mrs Carberry on his return, to convince her later, if necessary, that he had never left the house.

5

BODIES IN THE WOOD

Mrs Swift, Mrs Stemp and Peggy, grandmother, mother and daughter respectively, were driving through the Kent countryside on a blissful afternoon in the summer of 1932 with a well packed hamper in the boot. They were looking for somewhere to picnic.

A short distance along the road they pulled in and proceeded to make themselves at home in a cosy spot walled by brambles and bracken. Young Peggy and her grandmother, still seated in the car, spread napkins on their laps while Janie Stemp handed out the carefully wrapped packages.

"Oh, isn't it simply glorious!" said Mrs Stemp, handing a flask into the car. She stood back with her arms upstretched towards the sky in a gesture of joy. Then, abruptly, she jerked forward. A loud, distant bang reverberated through the trees. Janie Stemp dropped to her knees and fell flat on her face.

Peggy gaped in astonishment, then turned to her grandmother for some explanation. But even as Mrs Swift, at a total loss for what to say, turned her face towards her grandchild, she was catapulted forward. The old lady's head flew back. The force of the bullet tore through the base of her neck, lifting her off the seat. A second missile ripped through her shoulder, hurling her against the windscreen.

Peggy didn't have time to scream. She didn't have time to look round or take stock of the situation. She didn't have time to take cover. The bolt-action .303 rifle had already been reloaded. A single bullet entered Peggy's right arm and came to lodge in her chest. Unlike her mother and grandmother, death for Peggy would not be instantaneous.

Did the young girl see the killer as he hauled off the body of his first victim, concealing it in the undergrowth? Did she see him stop whilst a lorry and a bus passed them by? Did she hear their car being driven 800 yards down the road and parked under the cover of some trees? If she did, it would have been the last sound she heard. Peggy was dead by the time the killer returned and dragged her body and the body of her mother on to a footpath.

The bodies lay there for some hours. Drivers on the road were unable to see them. Only when a bus went past, the 4.45 to Ashford, was the grisly crime discovered. From the upper deck William Daley, the conductor, clearly saw the body of a young girl. He stopped the bus and he and the driver, Ernest Randall, got out to investigate. They checked for vital signs, but none were present. Then they hastened to Boughton Lees to inform the police.

Nearly one hundred officers were involved in the manhunt that followed. A police bloodhound from West Sussex, recently used in a murder inquiry in Ruckinge, was brought in to assist and the public were asked to help.

The hunt for clues went on throughout the evening. Four miles from the scene a handbag containing £7.10s in notes was found. Detectives also found a shoe belonging to Mrs Swift, a partially eaten sandwich and Peggy's red beret.

It was about midnight when information was received which first put the police on the track of Private James Collins. He had been reported missing from the Hythe School of Musketry and had taken with him an army issue rifle and ammunition.

At this point there was not a great deal to connect him with the killings but, as the night wore on, police became ever more convinced that he was the man they were after.

Collins had deserted in the early hours of the morning and, at around 10.15 a.m., had been seen walking along the roads around Ashford. One witness mentioned that he was carrying a rifle, another that he had struck up a conversation with two women.

And then, at about 1 o'clock in the morning, a report came in from north London of a policeman being threatened with a gun.

Whilst patrolling on his bicycle, P.C. Chapman had spotted a soldier in Cockfosters Road. He was curious about the package the soldier was carrying, although he was not aware at the time that he had found the triple murderer. When questioned, Collins produced the rifle and pointed it at the policeman. Chapman tried to engage him in conversation, hoping, perhaps, that if he got the man's confidence he would be able to grab the rifle. But, after about 20 minutes, the soldier had darted into the bushes and disappeared.

By 2 a.m. there were some 200 officers in the area, some of them using tracker dogs. But Collins still evaded capture. He wasn't seen again until an observant patrolman located him on the outskirts of Barnet. He followed him on his motorcycle to a field in the Hadley Wood area.

Bravely, patrolman Reedman ordered the soldier to drop his rifle. Collins threatened him and, for a moment, the patrolman wondered if he would become the assassin's fourth victim. But, then, other officers had joined in the chase. Collins fired a number of shots into the air to keep them at bay, and this was the moment Reedman had been waiting for. With the killer's attention distracted, he charged at the soldier, knocking his rifle to the ground. Collins offered no further resistance, merely saying: "That's about the lot."

Private James Thomas Collins was formally charged with three murders at 9 a.m. on Wednesday, June 15th, 1932.

At the hearing the following week, Collins expressed bitter regret. "I am terribly sorry," he said. "It is a diabolical thing. No regrets of mine can ever be enough." But the soldier was never able to explain his actions. "I had my rifle with me. I cannot remember what happened afterwards, but they were killed and no doubt I did it."

The husbands of Mrs Swift and Mrs Stemp were called to give evidence. When asked if they knew the defendant, they both said they had never seen him before in their lives. Thomas Stemp added quietly: "I would like to have half an hour with him."

When the trial was over a verdict of guilty but insane was returned by the jury and Collins was ordered to be detained during His Majesty's pleasure. The police officers involved in the arrest were commended for their bravery.

The Ashford road is comparatively quiet these days. At the top of Challock Hill, picnickers still park their cars to admire the view and gaze with blissful ignorance of the shocking events that occurred there on one fateful summer's day.

6

THE CHARING CROSS
TRUNK MURDER

One afternoon in May 1927, a large black leather- covered trunk of American manufacture was deposited in the left-luggage office at London's Charing Cross Station. There was nothing exceptional about it, nothing the least bit worthy of notice. True, it was strange that a shoe shine boy had found the deposit ticket screwed up into a ball and thrown away. But, as the left-luggage attendant observed when the ticket was handed in: "People aren't as careful as they used to be. They just don't care any more."

The trunk stayed at Charing Cross for two days, attracting no more attention than any of the numerous other trunks that had been left at the office. On the third day, however, it began to make its presence felt. It began to smell. At first it was a gentle, inoffensive smell that was hardly noticeable amidst the smoke from the trains and the hurly burly of the station. But as the hours rolled by the smell became more and more pungent.

By the fourth day the smell could not be ignored. A horrible, sickening, all-pervading stench. It filled the office, it even attracted the attention of the travellers outside who were hurrying past to catch their trains. By lunchtime the staff at the left-luggage office could stand it no longer. They lugged the trunk from its rack, hauled it into a corner of the room and called for the police.

Divisional Detective Inspector Steele made his way from

Bow Street police station, accompanied by a detective sergeant. Armed with a knife and a pair of bolt cutters, they cut the straps and prized open the lock. Throwing back the lid, the two officers were confronted by the trunk's grisly contents. Staring up at them, with sightless eyes, was the head of a murdered woman.

Steele slammed the lid shut before the station staff could glimpse the horrific sight. He then called his headquarters to have the trunk removed and its ghoulish contents examined.

The trunk was duly transported to the mortuary where, under the watchful eye of Sir Bernard Spilsbury, the eminent Home Office pathologist, its contents were taken out. The woman's head lay on top. Underneath this, in four brown paper packages tied up with string, was the rest of her body. It had been neatly cut into quarters, each part still covered in its appropriate clothing.

Decomposition had already begun, hence the smell, but Spilsbury was still able to make something of it. He estimated that the woman had died on May 4th, two days before the body had been dumped in the trunk at Charing Cross. Death appeared to have been due to asphyxia, probably by pressure over the mouth and nose after a blow to the right temple had rendered her unconscious.

The clothing was now separated out in the hope that it would give some hint as to the woman's identity. It included a short skirt and a coat of grey tweed, a blue knitted jumper, a pair of salmon-coloured stockings and a vest. There was also a pair of shoes and a handbag. None of these bore any marks of identification. But, on the woman's dove-grey woollen knickers there was a name, P. Holt, woven into them in blue block letters. There was also a laundry mark in black ink.

Police published details of the trunk, the laundry mark and the name "P. Holt" in the national press and, as a result, a Mrs P. Holt from Redcliffe Gardens, Fulham, came forward. She examined the undergarments and confirmed that they were indeed hers and that they had been missing for some time. They had disappeared from her home after a woman she had engaged as cook, a Mrs Roles, had left her employ the previous August. Mrs Holt agreed to go to the mortuary to try and identify the dismembered body. "Yes," she said, in a state of some nervousness, "that is Mrs Roles."

Through a domestic agency which had secured Mrs Roles the position at Mrs Cook's home, it was discovered that the cook was, in reality, a certain Minnie Alice Bonati, aged 36, the estranged wife of an Italian waiter. Quickly, the police traced the waiter to a Baker Street restaurant, but he could give them little help. His wife, he said, had left him in 1923 after a row.

Meanwhile the publicity which the case was attracting brought forward some other leads. The trunk itself was recognised by a second-hand dealer on the Brixton Road who remembered selling it to a man of about 40, with a closely-cut dark moustache and a military bearing. A bus conductor remembered picking up a passenger near the shop on May 5th. He was carrying a large black trunk. Better still, a taxi driver recalled that, on or about May 6th, he had been hailed by a man with a heavy black trunk in the doorway of a house in Rochester Row. He had taken him, and his trunk, to Charing Cross.

Further information had also now been gleaned from the contents of the trunk itself. After the clothing found inside had been microscopically examined and photographed, Chief Inspector Cornish gave instruction that each article should be thoroughly washed in boiling water. One of the last items found wrapped around the remains in the trunk was a bloodstained yellow check duster. When this was thoroughly washed, it revealed the name of an hotel: The Greyhound.

Unfortunately it was the name used by scores of hotels throughout the country and many in London. But a check at each one eventually established that it had come from Fulham.

A barmaid whom the officers spoke to there recognised

it. She thought she might have taken it away in error.

The woman gave her name as Mrs John Robinson but explained that she was no longer living with her husband. She told the detectives that Mr Robinson ran a business in Rochester Row, and also gave a brief description of him. When they heard that he had a closely-cut moustache they were very anxious to make his acquaintance. They met him later that day at the Elephant and Castle.

John Robinson didn't seem concerned by the approach of the police officers and, indeed, appeared eager to give them what help he could. But he couldn't help much. He knew no Mrs Bonati, he had never owned a large black trunk and he had never deposited anything like a trunk at Charing Cross Station.

He willingly accepted the ordeal of an identification parade and seemed not the least anxious when confronted by the taxi-driver, the attendant at the left-luggage office and the dealer who had sold the trunk. And his innocence appeared to be vindicated when none of these men recognised him.

But Chief Inspector Cornish was still convinced that Robinson was his man and ordered an immediate search of his premises at 86 Rochester Row.

The rooms seemed to be neat and tidy. There were no bloodstains on the walls or floor, no broken furniture, no smashed glass. Nothing, in fact, to indicate that anything remotely untoward had ever happened there. But then the officers tipped out the contents of a waste-bucket. At first glance, it appeared to contain nothing unusual. But closer inspection showed that one matchstick was a different colour to the others. It looked as if it was bloodstained.

This matchstick was later analysed and, indeed, the stains were shown to be blood. Moreover, it was of the same blood group as that of Mrs Bonati. It was a flimsy piece of evidence. In itself it was nothing much. But it was enough to shake Robinson's confidence. He now told detectives all that they wanted to hear.

On May 23rd, 1927, John Robinson was charged with

murder. On July 12th, at his trial at the Old Bailey, Robinson went into the witness box and told his story,

He said that he had met Minnie Bonati on May 4th outside the Post Office close to his office. They had chatted for a while and she had propositioned him. They both went back to his office and he sat and wrote some letters. After a while, he turned to the woman and then she suddenly demanded money. When he refused to pay, she became very angry and abusive. He told her to go away, but she raised her hand as if to strike him.

"I threw her head back, knocking a pane out of the window," Robinson said. "I hit her and she fell.

"I told her, 'Get out as quickly as you can, I am off,' and I left the office. Next day, when I returned, she was still lying on the floor - but she was dead.

"I sat down to review the position and arrived at the conclusion that I had better find some means of disposing of the body. I decided to cut it up and went out and bought some string and paper and a knife."

After cutting up the body, he said, he bought the trunk. On the following day, he packed the woman's remains into it and took it to Charing Cross Station. On the next day - the 7th - he "straightened up the office and waited for clients."

Robinson's story was all right as far as it went, but it failed to explain how the woman had been asphyxiated.

Officers believed that after striking Mrs Bonati in his office, he held a cushion over her mouth and nose to stifle her screams and had suffocated her. Then he calmly and deliberately formulated his plan for disposing of her body.

It was mentioned during the trial that, shortly after his arrest, Robinson had accompanied the police to Clapham Common where, under a tree which he pointed out, they had found a large chef's knife partially buried. Its blade was one foot long.

The jury refused to accept Robinson's plea that the death was accidental and, on June 14th, after an absence of two hours, they found him guilty of murder.

John Robinson was hanged at Pentonville on August 12th, 1927.

7

THE FLYING KILLER AND THE KIDNAPPED BEAUTY

It was the summer of 1939. The sky was blue and the sun was shining. The sleek two-seater aeroplane made a bumpy landing in the field outside Vernon, Illinois, but Pletch judged it a success. Indeed, for a man with next to no flying experience it was something of a triumph. And yet all was not well. Ernest Pletch might have got down to the ground, but the 29-year-old adventurer had no money and he was nearly out of fuel. He wondered what he could do next.

In a short while, however, salvation was at hand. A crowd of several people had gathered around the plane and they were all gazing at it with interest. Among the crowd was mining executive John Gehrken, his attractive wife and their pretty 17-year-old daughter, Goldie.

Pletch jumped out of the plane and introduced himself to the onlookers. He said his name was Larry Thompson and he was a former army pilot on a barnstorming tour.

"How much do you charge?" Mr Gehrken asked.

"A dollar a passenger."

"We'll all go," said the mining executive.

"I'd rather stay on the ground," his pretty daughter insisted with a laugh.

The young adventurer turned on all his charm, but the girl remained resolute. So Thompson took each of her parents for a ride. And, more importantly, got them down safely.

Other passengers appeared and, by nightfall, the flyer had a modest roll of dollar bills in his pocket.

He accepted the Gehrkens' invitation to dine with them and to remain overnight as their guest. He was fascinated by the young Goldie. She, in her turn, was enthralled by his tales of adventure - especially his daredevil accounts of flying for the military. From what he said, Larry Thompson was certainly an experienced flyer and a courageous one too.

As the evening wore on Goldie finally yielded to his entreaties to accompany him in the skies. She promised Pletch that she would go for a ride in the plane the following morning.

Goldie got her ride. But, instead of landing after a short hop, Mr and Mrs Gehrken watched in alarm as the plane carrying their daughter disappeared swiftly over the horizon.

Details of the abduction were soon splashed across the front pages of the Mid-Western newspapers, and Pletch was hailed as the "Flying Romeo." Police, however, were unwilling to treat the crime so lightly. They knew that Pletch had already had criminal convictions both for theft and forgery. They also knew that the plane had been stolen. They were seriously concerned about his passenger's safety.

As it turned out, however, Goldie Gehrken came to no harm. She was found two days later on a farm in Wyatt, Missouri, where Pletch was again busy taking passengers for dollar rides. She looked well and insisted that Pletch had taken excellent care of her. She said he had treated her like "a real princess." "He kept begging me to marry him," she joked coquettishly, "but I wouldn't't."

Relieved by the happy outcome of the drama, Goldie's parents decided to drop their charge of kidnapping. Instead, a warrant was issued charging Pletch with aeroplane theft and, under $500 bail, the daring young man was released.

In the months before his trial Pletch made much of his exploits in the air, boasting to all and sundry: "I'm Pletch - the fellow who stole an aeroplane, kidnapped that girl and flew all over the country." He also embarked on marriage, his third, to a pretty twenty- three year-old, Frances Bales. Pletch seemed to be without a care in the world.

But then, on the morning of Wednesday, October 25th, the day he was due to appear in court to plead guilty, Ernest Pletch disappeared. He could not be found anywhere. An investigation revealed that he had stolen his sister's 1932 Ford V-8 coupé. In addition he had made off with his father's shotgun, a quantity of ammunition, thirty gallons of gasoline and a radio.

"We're afraid he's up to something desperate," his anxious father declared, "He's never shown the slightest interest in weapons before."

Pletch arrived at Brookfield airport early on Thursday afternoon. He was greeted by a wiry, sandy-haired man in his late thirties.

"My name's Carl Bivens," the man said, "I'm the instructor here."

"I'm Larry Thompson," said Pletch, "I want to do some flying. I've had some time, but I want to solo."

"Have you got a student permit?" asked Bivens.

Pletch frowned at the inevitable question. "No," he answered.

"Well," said the pilot, "I can give you instruction, but I can't let you solo."

"That's all right," said Pletch reasonably. "I'll get one when I need it."

"When do you want to start?"

"Right away."

A brand new Cub sport model was wheeled out and the two men took their seats, Pletch in the rear, Bivens in the front. They took off from the small airport and spiralled upwards. Soon they were soaring through the clouds.

It took less than five minutes for the pilot to realize that his student was no novice. He cut the throttle and yelled:

"You fly all right. Take her over." Pletch did as he was told.

At 5.35 p.m. the following Saturday, Metallus Clay and Harry Williams watched with interest as a small yellow monoplane circled lazily in the calm, late afternoon sky, then settled to a smooth landing in a nearby pasture.

"He's landed on Meredith Dillman's place," Clay observed. "I wonder if there's something wrong?"

A car carrying a neighbour, Miss Ruth Koontz, drew up beside the young men. The girl also had seen the plane land. Her radio was playing loudly and she appeared excited. "Maybe that's the fellow the police are looking for," she called.

"What fellow?" asked Clay.

When the girl explained, Clay said: "We'll look him over."

The two men trudged across the field and found a red-haired young man nervously pacing around the plane.

"Having trouble?" Williams asked.

"I had to come down on account of the darkness," said the pilot.

Pletch then asked them where he could buy something to eat. Williams directed him to the Clear Creek's general store. "Bill Wampler will fix you up," he added.

On reaching his home, Clay told his mother about the plane and what Ruth Koontz had said about it. She promptly called the operator, and repeated what her son had told her. The operator called Bloomington police.

"Can you get the plane's licence number?" the desk sergeant inquired.

"I'll try," replied the operator.

She called the Dillman farm and learned that the plane bore the number NC-24796, the same licence number as Bivens' missing Cub.

Pletch was picked up outside Wampler's general stores at 5.45 p.m. Handcuffs were slipped on his wrists and he was searched. The officers found a loaded .32 calibre revolver, a box of ammunition, a wrist-watch, Carl Bivens's commercial pilot's licence and $14.60 in cash.

Examination of the interior of the plane revealed bloodstains on the handle of the horizontal stabiliser control and on the floor. Later, Carl Bivens' body was found concealed in a hedge a mile from the point were Pletch had landed. Bivens had been shot. There was blood all over his jacket.

At first Pletch tried to convince the police that it had all been an accident. He launched into a tale about a fight in mid-air. He claimed that Bivens's body had wedged the controls and sent the plane into a dive. "I had to fire the second time to relax his body," he said, "I pulled out - at 1,500 feet."

No one believed a word of it and a police reconstruction proved that it was false. They conjectured that, far from acting in self defence, Pletch had calmly fired two bullets into the back of Carl Bivens's head, killing him instantly,

On Sunday afternoon the murderer's grief-stricken parents and his sister were allowed to see him. The visit was a short one. "Pray, Ernest," his weeping mother advised. "That's all there is left."

Pletch alone failed to shed any tears.

Pletch's father expressed his sorrow to Etta Bivens, the slain aviator's widow. "His mother and I would gladly see him dead if we could undo this terrible deed."

Mrs Bivens expressed her sympathy for the killer's parents and said, "I sincerely hope your son will not be sent to the gas chamber. I'll be satisfied to know that he is put away for ever."

Pleading guilty to Carl Bivens's murder, Ernest Pletch appeared calm, even jaunty, as the judge asked: "In view of the fact that I am about to mete out to you the lesser of two punishments for your crime, do you swear that you will never seek parole?"

Pletch agreed to the undertaking.

Sentenced to imprisonment for the duration of his life, Ernest Pletch is believed to be the first man in criminal history to be convicted of committing a murder while in flight in an aeroplane.

8

THE PIOUS MURDERESS
OF PARIS

It took Elodie Ménétret just one month to decide that she didn't like her new housekeeper. She had met the woman in a shop in the Boulevard Haussmann and, at the time, had thought she was rather pleasant. But now, having the woman living under the same roof in her beautiful house in Villemomble, Elodie realized she had made a dreadful mistake.

Euphrasie Mercier was 18 years her senior. She was tall, with a wrinkled face, a hooked nose and a sharp manner. Hauntings and crimes were her favoured topics of conversation and she was forever telling Elodie stories of how solitary women were easy targets for murderers and thieves.

"I'm terribly worried," she confessed to her old friend Pierre Grassier, "I've tried to dismiss Euphrasie but she obstinately refuses to go. She says she just wants food and lodgings but I really don't want her to stay. She frightens me."

Grassier agreed to come by the house in a few days and see what he could do. He suggested that, in any case, he could collect Elodie's valuables and securities for safe keeping."

On April 18th, 1883, Elodie and a neighbour, Mlle Grière, drew up a duplicate list of her securities, deeds and jewellery. Seven days later, as he had agreed, Pierre Grassier made his call.

When he reached her home, however, he found the building shuttered and silent. And it remained that way for some days. When it finally returned to something closer to normality he still had no luck. Now, whenever he called, he was always put off.

It wasn't just M. Grassier who had become unwanted. Whenever any visitors came to the house they would be turned away. "Mlle Ménétret is dead to the world," Euphrasie would inform them. "She has entered a convent and I have sworn not to divulge the place of her retreat."

Mlle Louise Ménétret, a niece of Elodie's, was no more successful than anyone else in solving the mystery of her aunt's whereabouts. She, too, received the stock answer: "She's in a convent."

Elodie's niece found this hard to believe so she went to the Commissary of Police in Montreuil and told him she suspected all was not well. As a consequence he summoned Euphrasie to appear before him. Extraordinarily, however, he was quite satisfied when she produced a letter from Elodie which simply bore the date "Wednesday evening" and gave no address. He was equally trusting when Euphrasie produced a document which she claimed had been written by Elodie. It read: "I'm leaving France I leave all to Mlle Mercier let her transact my affairs." The handwriting was shaky, but he assumed it was authentic. The matter was not taken any further.

This episode must have filled the old woman with confidence. She was certainly happy with the result and, very shortly afterwards, became even more audacious.

In August 1883, Euphrasie journeyed to Luxembourg. She visited a notary and claimed that she was herself Elodie Ménétret. She explained that she had come to stay in Luxembourg and, having property at Villemomble, near Paris, she wanted to draw up a power of attorney in favour of a friend, Mlle Euphrasie Mercier, who was to administer the estate.

The notary told Mlle Ménétret that the papers she had brought with her were not sufficient on their own and that she would also have to produce two witnesses who could prove her identity. Euphrasie went out and within half an hour was back with the required witnesses - a musician and a hairdresser - who for five francs each were only too pleased to swear that the lady was indeed Elodie Ménétret and she had been known to them for years. The notary was satisfied with the statement and the document was drawn up.

Now, with the fraudulent power of attorney, Euphrasie returned to Villemomble and began to sell off most of the furniture and belongings. She also collected some rent money which an uncle of Elodie's regularly paid, and even reminded a former lover of Elodie's that he was honour bound to keep up his monthly payment of 125 francs.

This bizarre situation continued for two whole years. But for the gossip in the village, it might have gone on considerably longer. Once the rumours started to circulate, however, the end of Euphrasie's curious fantasy was inevitably in sight.

Euphrasie employed a gardener whom she forced to work in a rather eccentric manner. He had strict orders to keep the garden gates shut. Euphrasie said she didn't want stray dogs coming in and scratching up her flowerbeds. One flower bed in particular, she commanded, had to be treated with special care. It contained a mass of dahlias and woe betide anyone who let a dog roam across it. In fact, woe betide anyone who went near it, This was Euphrasie's special patch which only she was allowed to tend. Even the gardener had to keep away from it.

Before long the authorities got wind of the stories that were being told about this flower bed. Most of them seemed unlikely, some of them seemed absurd. But eventually they felt compelled to act. There were just too many rumours to ignore. A search of Mlle Ménétret's garden was ordered and Mlle Mercier's prized flower bed was dug up.

The dahlias were uprooted to reveal underneath some burnt clothing, a pile of charred bones and a number of teeth, one of which had been filled with gold. They were immediately sent off for analysis.

Medical experts said the bones were those of a woman of 45 - the approximate age of Elodie Ménétret. An expert gardener, examining the dahlia roots and other bulbs, thought they must have been taken out of the ground and replaced in the spring of 1883 - when Elodie vanished. Elodie's dentist confirmed that he had filled one of her teeth with gold.

Euphrasie Mercier was arrested for murder.

She protested her innocence loudly and firmly. She insisted that Elodie was alive and well and living in a convent. The bones, she said, meant nothing. The garden was an old cemetery. Futhermore, she claimed that her old mistress had never been her mistress at all and the house was really her own. So what did she have to benefit from the murder?

In court, Euphrasie insisted that God, her eternal comfort, had dictated all her actions, including various business and property transactions. She said it was she and not Elodie Ménétret who had bought the house at Villemomble. She had obtained it with her own money - strictly at God's direction - to serve her as a retreat before going on a religious pilgrimage.

"But," interposed the judge, "it was Mlle Ménétret who paid for it."

"With 15,000 francs I had lent her," retorted Euphrasie.

"Have you a receipt?" Judge Dubard asked.

"No, I don't understand business."

"Were you not in fact her servant?"

"We had agreed to let it appear so. I wanted to keep my pecuniary circumstances a secret from my family, whom I had been keeping all my life. I was getting old and I wanted to reserve a part of my savings for God."

"Found among your papers was a receipt which Elodie Ménétret signed for the 15,000 francs you had supposedly lent her. Unfortunately for you, that receipt, dated 1878, was written on legal paper with the date 1882 on the watermark. Presumably you forged a signature left behind by Mlle Ménétret."

Euphrasie replied stolidly: "The receipt is completely genuine."

After claiming that it was she who had advised Elodie to entrust her deeds and valuables to M. Grassier, Euphrasie gave her version of Elodie's disappearance.

"She made up her mind to flee the world. She was in love with a man whom she could not marry. She worshipped him as the angels love. Besides, she was afraid to live in the house - sinister types had been seen prowling round the walls. One evening she threw herself at the feet of a priest and the next day, after spending all night burning her letters, she left."

"That is your version," commented the judge. "You are aware, however, of what the prosecution allege? They say that Elodie Ménétret never left the house, that she was buried there, and that you murdered her."

"Impossible!" Euphrasie shrieked. "I, who wouldn't hurt a cat or a rabbit! To kill a poor lady I loved so dearly!"

"In that case, where is she?" demanded the judge.

"I don't know."

"You have given many and various accounts of her whereabouts. You have said she was in Paris, in Belgium, then in Luxembourg and Mecklenburg."

"She often changed her convent. I have seen her in the habits of different sisterhoods. She used to write to me."

"Where are the letters?"

"I sent them all back to her by her own orders. She was dead to the world and was afraid least any indiscretion should divulge her place of retreat."

"Have you seen her?"

"Often."

"Where?"

"At night once, for instance, under the clock at the Gare du Nord."

The judge snorted. "Do you know of any convent where they would tolerate such escapades?"

Euphrasie was silent.

Euphrasie Mercier's trial went on for four days. Throughout that time she consistently protested her innocence. She stuck with her account of the events even though no one in the courtroom could believe her.

It took 90 minutes for the jury to find her guilty of murder, and also of charges of forgery and theft. She was sentenced to the maximum term of imprisonment for one of her age - 20 years.

9

PROUD TO BE A MURDERER

At 9.15 p.m. on Saturday, April 17th, 1954, 75-year-old window-cleaner Bertram Chaplin was drinking at The Gunmakers, a cosy little pub in Lichfield Road, Aston, when he saw three of his pals huddled over a table across the room. Giving a small belch and wiping his foam-flecked lips with the back of his hand, Chaplin picked up his glass and walked over to join them.

"'Ello, Bertram," said Samuel Plant, moving his chair round to make room for the newcomer. "Come an' sup wi' us."

Chaplin said nothing, but took his seat. Then, with a broad smile on his face, he made the announcement his friends would never forget.

"Today", he said, "I am going to cause the biggest sensation in Aston."

His friends looked bemused.

"What do you mean?" asked Plant.

"I've done her in!" he declared, playfully moving his glass around in circles on the table.

"You mean Annie?"

"Yes," said Chaplin in a matter of fact way. "Who else would I mean?"

There was a stunned silence. Chaplin gulped down the last of his beer. "And now," he said, putting down his glass on the table, "I am going to the police."

With that he stood up, turned and strode purposefully out of the pub with not even a backward glance.

It was 10 p.m. when Chaplin swaggered up to the duty-sergeant's counter at Victoria Road police station to make his confession. "There is a dead woman in my house," he said cheerfully.

"Indeed?" said the officer, barely noticing his visitor and assuming that he was drunk. "Is there anyone else in the house?"

"No. Just the dead woman."

The duty officer duly entered the man's name and address in the station log book and summoned a senior officer. Shortly afterwards, Bertram Chaplin was bundled into a police car and driven home to 404 Victoria Road.

Chaplin unlocked the front door and led the way through the living-room to a passage into the scullery. He switched on the light. "There she is," he said. "I choked her."

Officers crowded around the woman, who was dressed in a fur coat and lying on the floor. Her face was bloated and her eyes bulged out from their sockets. Her tongue drooped down the side of her jaw, and there were drops of blood on her lips. The livid marks around her neck showed that she had been strangled. One of the officers who was new to the division walked to the corner of the room and retched. Another, with unnecessary concern for procedure, checked the body for vital signs. None were found.

Back at the police station and now under arrest, Bertram Chaplin was interviewed by Detective Inspector Renshaw in the presence of other officers and a stenographer. A uniformed constable stood guard by the door.

"All right now, Chaplin," Renshaw said, seating himself, "Take your time. Then, when you are ready, please tell us everything."

Renshaw didn't have to wait long for the suspect to speak.

"I done it. You can hang me tonight," said Chaplin simply. He held his arms out and showed his hands to the officers. They were large and square like shovels. "Look at these," he said, "They are the strongest hands in Aston. I choked her with them."

He smiled proudly.

Chaplin then embarked on a long litany of complaints about his former mistress. "I took her off the streets... She was in rags and I dressed her up and made her smart... I bought her a fur coat ... and I murdered her in it. I don't like liars. She thought she was clever, but she didn't reckon with Bert Chaplin."

When Chaplin's tirade had come to a close, Detective Inspector Renshaw formally charged him with murder. "Tonight I am the happiest man in England," was Chaplin's astonishing reply, "I have done a murder and I am proud of it."

On Monday, April 19th, Bertram Chaplin appeared in court at Birmingham charged with the unlawful killing of 47-year-old Mrs Ann Emms.

Mr M. P. Pugh, prosecuting, said that Mrs Emms had been living with the prisoner since August 9th, 1948 but their relationship had been very stormy.

Chaplin was a widower, he said, but the woman was married. She was the estranged wife of Harold Ernest Emms.

Later the court heard more of their uneasy love affair. They had frequent arguments and fights. From time to time Ann Emms would go back to her husband, but she would always return to live with Chaplin. Harold Emms said he noticed signs of violence against his wife - cuts and bruises - that had clearly been inflicted by the prisoner. Others testified that Chaplin had made threats against her. Chaplin's three friends from the pub also gave their evidence.

Evidence for the defence came from Dr James O'Reilly of Winson Green Mental Hospital. Dr O'Reilly said he considered Chaplin to be emotionally overactive, elated, boastful, talkative and with an undue sense of physical well-being. He was easily confused, and with regard to the crime, showed no emotional reaction at all. Neither did he appreciate the gravity of his position. In his opinion Chaplin had not known at the time of the murder that what he was doing was wrong.

Dr O'Reilly's testimony was backed up by the opinions of Dr Percy Coates, medical officer at Winson Green and Dr Arthur Huse, a specialist in mental diseases. Both agreed that Bertram Chaplin was suffering from organic dementia, which would affect his powers of judgement. At the time of the murder, Chaplin knew the nature and quality of his act, but he did not know that what he was doing was wrong.

The jury was out for just 35 minutes before returning a verdict of guilty but insane. The judge directed that Chaplin should be detained at Broadmoor until the Queen's pleasure be known.

10

THE MESMERIC INFLUENCE OF ZADRAZIL THE KILLER

On New Year's Eve, 1931, Francizka Wachauf and Frau Hopflinger, her elderly landlady, were sitting comfortably by the fire in the Villa Irma, Frau Hopflinger's charming holiday home at Gresshubl near Vienna, Austria, when their peace was suddenly interrupted by a loud knock at the door.

The young woman went to answer it and returned with a tall, slender man who had fair hair and deep-set, penetrating eyes. Francizka introduced him as her lawyer, Dr Kalman.

Dr Kalman greeted Frau Hopflinger and asked if he might look over the villa with her. "I need to make certain it is in proper order for my client, Fräulein Wachauf, to rent."

Francizka seemed embarrassed. "I'm sure everything is all right," she ventured.

Her lawyer ignored the remark.

"What about the heating system?" he enquired.

The elderly owner looked at the man in astonishment. "I can assure you that the heating system is in perfect working order," she said, "Come, I'll show it to you. It's in the basement."

Francizka was still beside the fire when she heard a muffled cry. She rushed out into the hall and down the stairs. As she reached the huge vaulted basement her face paled. Just visible above the top of the bath in one corner of the room were the head and shoulders of her landlady. Frau Hopflinger's wrinkled face was transfixed with horror and she was trembling violently.

Francizka tried to scream, but no sound came out.

"Take this gun," said the man, thrusting the weapon into her right hand. "Keep her covered. I'll be upstairs."

Francizka nodded obediently. She did exactly as she was ordered. Standing before her landlady, the gun in her hand, she remained there for what seemed like hours.

Finally the man returned, this time with a new set of orders. He snatched the gun away from Francizka and stuffed a large white handkerchief into her hands.

"Bandage her eyes!" he commanded.

Without a murmur, Francizka walked towards the bath. The old woman made no sound as the blindfold was tied around her. Then Francizka turned around and began to walk away. As she did so a shot rang out. A second shot quickly followed and Frau Hopflinger slumped in the tub.

The man then grabbed Francizka by the shoulder. "Now it's your turn!" he barked.

Desperately Francizka fought her attacker. She almost broke free before he caught her by the arm, swung her around and fired a shot. The young woman staggered. Then another bullet was fired into her head. She collapsed on the floor.

Three hours later the New Year's celebration at the Hobls Inn, a short distance away from the villa, was brought to a sudden close when a bloodstained woman stumbled through the door. "I'm Francizka Wachauf," she gasped, "shot at the Villa Irma!" The words ended in a low moan as Francizka's consciousness finally gave out.

The young woman was swiftly taken to hospital where doctors expressed scant hope of saving her life.

In the meantime detectives from Vienna were busy trying to solve the mystery. They had already found the body of Frau Hopflinger and had searched the villa in case the killer was still lurking somewhere within. To their surprise, most of the house was neat and tidy. Just two of its rooms had been ransacked. Later, however, they discovered that Frau Hopflinger's apartment home in Vienna had also been robbed, and here the thieves had been much more thorough. Significantly, they had gained access with a key. Was it for this key that the old lady had been killed?

Detectives began to investigate the background of Franzizka Wachauf. They discovered that, until a week before, she had been living in a furnished room in Vienna. She had had few friends but was in love with a young man named Victor Klein. The couple had rented a villa in the country and would probably marry and live there.

Her Viennese landlady's description of Herr Klein, which stressed the mysterious look in his eyes, was circulated to all newspapers with the request that anybody with information should come forward.

The next day an attractive woman, clutching a newspaper under one arm, walked into police headquarters.

"I think I can help you find Victor Klein," she announced.

Inspector Alois Brunnhuber, who was heading the enquiry, brought her immediately into his room.

"Do you know Klein?" he asked.

"Yes, I think I do - but not under that name." The woman fumbled in her handbag and brought out a photograph which she handed to the detective. "I believe that man is your Victor Klein. I knew him as Victor Zadrazil."

"What makes you think this man is Klein?" asked the officer.

"Zadrazil was in love with me until about a month ago when he found another girl and left me," she said. "I tried to find him, but couldn't. I did learn, however, that the girl's name was Franzizka and that Victor dominated her completely. He dominated me too, for a time."

The young woman gazed into space, then she added thoughtfully, "There's some strange power behind Victor's eyes."

"What do you mean by that?" Brunnhuber asked.

"I don't know exactly, but I believe he can hypnotise women."

"I see," said the inspector with some scepticism. He then thanked the lady for her help, dismissed her and issued orders for his detectives to find Victor Zadrazil and bring him in. The girl had supplied an address where the man had lived during the time she had known him.

Inspector Brunnhuber now made his way to the hospital where, against all expectations, Franczka Wachauf was making a slow recovery and had already regained consciousness. Placing the photograph before her, he waited expectantly for her reaction. For a while Franczka only stared, then suddenly her eyes went wild with fright. "That's Victor!" she shrieked.

By the time the inspector had returned to Vienna, Zadrazil had been brought in for questioning. Brunnhuber studied the tall young man carefully. He saw at a glance why women fell under his spell. Zadrazil's deep-set magnetic eyes stared back at the inspector almost insolently. The man had an extraordinary presence. He exuded an air of extreme confidence.

"I understand that you wish to question me in regard to the Hopflinger murder," he said calmly. "It will save us both time if I tell you at once that I have no knowledge of the affair. On the night in question I was riding in a taxi with my wife. There was an accident, which you will find recorded in the police files."

Picking up the telephone, Brunnhuber ordered an immediate check on the story. He was stunned by the result. According to the records Zadrazil had indeed been in Vienna at the time of Frau Hopflinger's murder. There was no way that he could have killed the old woman. "And yet," thought Brunnhuber, "I am absolutely certain that he did. So how did he manage it?"

Three hours later it was a much happier detective inspector who called Zadrazil back into his office.

"Zadrazil," he began, "your alibi was too perfect. When I looked into the accident report I found you had merely bumped your head on the roof of a taxi. Yet you insisted upon calling the police and having it recorded.

"We have also discovered that the woman who was with you - and who you stated was your wife - is in reality the wife of your brother.

"Furthermore, an hour ago Francizka Wachauf gave me all the details of how you killed Frau Hopflinger and shot her."

The young man stared at the inspector with contempt. "I suppose that you are prepared to prove your accusations," he said.

"Yes," replied Brunnhuber, "I am indeed. You deliberately had Francizka rent the Villa Irma to establish contact with the owner whom you planned to rob. It was you who suggested inviting the elderly woman to spend New Year's Eve in her own holiday villa. Francizka Wachauf was completely under your dominance. She introduced you as her lawyer as you had instructed her then guarded Frau Hopflinger while you raced back to the woman's apartment in Vienna. On the way, you picked up your sister-in-law and had the accident recorded in order to establish an alibi, then you left your brother's wife outside while you hurriedly went through the apartment. Your sister-in-law also seems to be under your spell, and did as you told her, saying she was your wife and agreeing with your account of how you had spent the evening."

"Forgive me," interrupted Zadrazil, "but you spoke of proof. All you have told me so far is speculation. You have only the word of these women against mine."

"My detectives have also located the taxi driver who has identified you as the man he drove from Frau Hopflinger's apartment to within five minutes walk of the Villa Irma," Brunnhuber continued. "He said you arrived there at about ten-thirty, the approximate time of the murder."

The prisoner now sank into the chair. His bravado evaporated. In the end Zadrazil made a full confession.

"Yes," he admitted, "It was as you say. I took Frau Hopflinger into the basement and made her give me the keys to her Vienna apartment, then got Francizka to watch her. I drove to Vienna, picking up my sister-in-law on the way. I got almost nothing from the apartment as the old woman kept her valuables in the bank safe.

"As you say I took another taxi, returned to the villa and shot the two women. Then I went back to Vienna, threw the gun into the river and told my brother's wife what she was to say. She knew nothing of the robbery and murder."

Thus was the crime revealed in all its dreadful details. Francizka Wachauf recovered. At a re-enactment of the tragedy, which took place two months later, the girl began to tremble, then fainted when confronted by Zadrazil.

At the trial in April 1932, she was given a sentence of only four years for her part in the crime, the jury believing that she had been hypnotised by the killer. However, Victor Zadrazil was sentenced to life imprisonment.

11

STAFFORDSHIRE'S DANCING SKELETON

Was William Hawkeswood a black magician? Was he in league with the devil? The residents of the small Staffordshire village of Pedmore certainly thought so. The lad had already been convicted of grave robbing, though he escaped with a caution, and now he was indulging in an even more sinister practice.

Still only a teenager, Hawkeswood began to amuse himself by fashioning a skeleton out of human bones and a skull and fitting it with wires and strings. It moved, rather like a puppet, and if any villager chanced to pass by Hawkeswood's residence at night, they would find themselves confronted by this eerie marionette, its bony arms outstretched beckoning them to come forward. Operating the skeleton from behind - and dressed entirely in black to blend in with the darkness - Hawkeswood would provide a suitably ghostly voice to complete the macabre illusion.

The effect of these antics on the folk of Pedmore was predictable. They simply refused to stand for it. Soon enough the entire Hawkeswood family were shunned and young William was forced to leave the area and move to nearby Swindon.

This was how William Hawkeswood came to arrive at Chasepool Lodge and found employment, first as a coachman and then as bailiff to Mr John Parker. He endeared himself to the staff no better than he had to the villagers of his old town. Sarah Sheldon, the 58- year-old housekeeper found him particularly odious. But his employer thought very differently indeed. Parker took an immediate liking to the young man. He found his new coachman intelligent, quick-witted and surprisingly knowledgeable in matters of health and medicine. The old man, who suffered from a stomach complaint, thought the camomile tea William made was particularly soothing.

On November 24th, however, the tea didn't taste quite the same. Sarah Sheldon had a sip of it in the kitchen and was sick. John Parker drank a whole cup and became very ill indeed. Within a week he was dead.

It didn't take long for people to suspect Hawkeswood and, when white mercury was found in the tea, his guilt seemed proven. Moreover it was discovered that he had bought the poison just the previous day.

Hawkeswood pleaded his innocence. He admitted to having purchased the white mercury - and also to putting some into Sarah Sheldon's tea. "She was always against me," he explained, "So I decided to teach her a lesson." But he said there was only enough in it to make her unwell and that there was none at all in his master's brew. He then reasoned that it must have been Sheldon who had killed John Parker. "I believe she realised what I had done and put mercury into the master's tea to spite me."

The jury was not impressed by Hawkeswood's logic. He was convicted and, on April 6th, 1808, sentenced to hang.

Hawkeswood's dead body was later cut down and conveyed to Swindon, where it was exhibited "as a warning to others." Many of the villagers who had been the victims of Hawkeswood's black humour turned out to see his broken body. They were there also, a few days later, at a lonely crossing on Chasepool Road, where his remains were eventually buried.

For years afterwards, people avoided that crossroads after dark. It was said to be haunted by a skeleton which walked along the road, beckoning unwary travellers to come forward.

12

THE EXMOOR MONSTER

The Reverend William Thornton knew that Burgess was a rogue. The scoundrel had already fooled him out of a guinea with a sob story that turned out to be a pack of lies. But the young parson was not one to bear grudges. Twenty-seven years old and eager to make a contribution to the bleak Exmoor parish of Simonsbath, Thornton was quick to make himself available when Burgess's need for help was real.

It was early in 1858 and William Burgess's wife had fallen ill with measles. This, combined with inflammation of the lungs, made her very sick indeed. In a matter of days, she was dead and the three Burgess children were left without a mother.

"My home has broken up, Parson," wailed Burgess, "My three children will have to go into service."

Thornton rushed into action and endeavoured to find homes for them all. It was no easy task. Nobody was disposed to foster these rough, ill-kempt children. Eventually, however, a family in New Molton agreed to take Tom and Emma. Anna, poor lass, was left out. She would have to go with her father.

Burgess supported Anna in his lodgings for one whole week, paying the two shillings and sixpence that was charged for her keep. By the end of those seven days, however, he had had enough. "Bundle up my kid's clothes," he told his landlady, "I'm taking her to lodge with her grannie in Porlock." The landlady did as she was bade and, shortly afterwards, father and daughter headed off out of the town.

Burgess returned that same evening, all alone. The following Thursday he told his landlady that he was moving to Porlock too.

All seemed well until a few days later when the remains of a burnt dress were found at the back of Burgess's old lodgings. The landlady was asked to inspect it. "It do belong to little Anna," she said, "It's her spare frock."

The following morning, almost afraid to put his uneasy suspicion into words, Thornton asked a local forester to go over to Porlock to see if old Mrs Burgess was well and if Anna and her father were safe. The forester agreed and soon set off. He came back with grim news. "Anna ain't there," he said, "and nor is Burgess."

Thornton was now close to panic. He was certain that Anna had been killed and he ordered an immediate search of the moor. "Look for a grave," he said tersely. The men from the parish grimly set about the task.

Thornton himself set of on horseback to ride the 40 miles to Cury Rivel and the home of Superintendent Jeffs. Hearing what he had to say, the chief of police was soon accompanying Thornton back to Simonsbath.

On the outskirts of the village, Thornton and Jeffs were met by a group of locals who had been waiting for them. "We've found the grave!" they said.

"Well, what else can you tell us?" Thornton wanted to know.

"It's empty," a woman informed them.

The grave was about a mile from Burgess's old lodgings, sited in a lane leading to the Wheal Eliza mine. It was just the right size for a child. It was almost certainly the one in which Anna's body had lain. But why was the grave now empty?

While Thornton was pondering this problem, William Burgess was arrested. Trying to flee Exmoor and make his way to Wales, he had been apprehended on a fishing boat to Swansea.

"What have you done with Anna?" Thornton demanded when the old rogue had been brought back to Simonsbath.

Burgess stared straight ahead in defiant silence. Thornton, overcome with irritation and weariness, snapped. "Murderer! How dare you remain silent? You are the worst of murderers!"

"That wasn't clever," the shrewd Jeffs told the parson quietly, "You've let him know we haven't found the body."

Thornton was chastened, but still defiant. "We'll find Anna's body yet. I swear we will."

In the months that followed, Thornton may have begun to regret his oath. The search continued everywhere, but still no body was found. And then a local poacher went to the vicarage, asking that what he had to tell the parson would be treated in confidence.

"We saw the grave, my mate and me," the man told Thornton, "and to be honest we reckoned a sheep had been buried to be picked up later. We decided to go back ourselves for the carcase when it was dark. We thought it would be a nice present for the wives. They could have cooked it up a treat."

"Who else have you told about this?" the parson asked.

The man hesitated.

"William Burgess," he eventually replied, "We was going to share it, the carcase, all three of us."

Thornton's mind raced. So that was it. Burgess had been told by the poachers about their supposed find and, knowing that it was not a sheep's carcase, he knew what he had to do. He had to disinter his daughter's body.

"We agreed to meet Burgess after dark to dig up the sheep carcase," the man went on. "But Burgess never turned up, so we reckoned we'd better leave things be."

"Is that all?" Thornton asked.

"Well, sir, not exactly. Later that night I was still out when someone passed below me going towards Wheal Eliza mine. I couldn't see who it was, though."

There was no doubt in Thornton's mind now. Where better to hide a body than down a disused mine shaft? The parson raced to the police and, they, in turn, acted with commendable speed. They invited tenders for the drainage of the shaft. The lowest price for clearing the 360 feet depth of water was £350. It was accepted with alacrity.

A volunteer was lowered into the shaft as Thornton and Fry waited anxiously at the top. Then there was a tug on the rope. The young man was pulled up and stepped clear.

In his arms he carried a piece of old tarpaulin tied up with thick cord. He handed the parcel to Thornton who cut the cord with his knife. All that remained of Anna Burgess lay there. Her corpse was wrapped in a little dress.

Burgess was tried at Somerset Assizes and sentenced to death. The jury were seen to be weeping as they brought in the verdict of guilty.

William Burgess was publicly hanged at Taunton Gaol on the stoke of 9 o'clock on January 4th, 1859. He struggled violently at the end of the rope but, in about a minute, he was dead.

13

DR CRIPPEN:
DEATH HAS NO TERROR FOR ME

On July 13th, 1910, a few lines of cold print told the public that the police had made a grim and ghastly discovery in the cellar of 39 Hilldrop Crescent, Camden Road, London. Under the cellar floor and steps they had found a quantity of pieces of skin and flesh, sundry internal organs, a few fragments of clothing, strands of hair, and a lady's curler. The flesh was buried in quicklime. No bones could be traced amongst the remains, and search as they might, they failed to uncover a head, hands or feet.

39 Hilldrop Crescent was the home of one Hawley Harvey Crippen, a doctor trained in America but unqualified to practise in his adopted London. He had already attracted police attention because of the disappearance of his wife some months earlier. Now, with the grisly discovery in his basement, they were more than eager to speak to the good doctor again.

Crippen's wife, Cora, who preferred to be known by her stage name of Belle Elmore, had last been seen on January 31st. That evening she and her husband had entertained two of her music-hall friends, Mr and Mrs Martinetti, to dinner at their home. It had been a pleasant enough affair, and nothing out of the ordinary happened. But the following day Cora had vanished. She was nowhere to be seen.

Crippen explained, to anyone who cared to listen, that his wife had left England for America where some theatrical opportunity had presented itself. Later he made it known that she was ill. None of her friends heard anything from her directly but, evidently, her health was deteriorating fast. Soon she was dead. On March 26th, a brief obituary notice appeared in the columns of Era magazine. It was greeted with shock.

Members of the Musical Hall Ladies' Guild, of which Belle Elmore had acted as honorary treasurer, pressed for further information concerning the death of their colleague and were dissatisfied with her husband's replies. They decided to contact Scotland Yard and ask them to investigate the matter.

Inspector Walter Dew subsequently interviewed Dr Crippen who admitted that the story of his wife's death was incorrect. The true version, he said, was that they had quarrelled and, in a fit of bad temper, Belle Elmore had left him. He had not seen her since. Crippen gave the detective full permission to search the house for any clues which might lead to his tracing his missing wife's whereabouts, an invitation Dew and his fellow officers readily accepted.

They were not surprised to find nothing untoward. Crippen's story, they thought, was not in the least implausible. It was clear to everyone that his marriage was far from happy and arguments were not uncommon. These rows, however, were usually rather one-sided. Cora had dominated her husband completely, cajoling him into buying her expensive gifts and demanding that he attended to the household chores. Any policeman who saw this mild-mannered, small framed man, with his drooping moustache and gold-rimmed spectacles, would have immediately recognised him as the down-trodden husband that he was. That his wife had left him was no great shock.

The officers were probably even amused when they saw a new young lady, Ethel le Neve, bustling about the house. His wife may have deserted him but the pathetic little man had landed on his feet. They assured Crippen that they would try and locate his wife, following the one lead he had given them that she may have run off with her old lover, the

American ex-prizefighter, Bruce Millar. They then made their apologies, and left.

However, when a few days later, Dr Crippen, in the company of Miss Ethel, suddenly disappeared, police suspicions were promptly re-awakened. Perhaps the little man had duped them after all. Orders were given to make a far more thorough search of his home. It was during that search that the grisly human remains were found.

A frantic hunt for the doctor and his companion began and, after a few long days of excitement in chasing false clues, the two were discovered. They were aboard the Canada bound steamer Montrose, where Miss le Neve had dressed herself as a boy to avoid identification. Captain Kendall became suspicious of the couple's affectionate behaviour towards each other and used the ship's radio to alert the police at Scotland Yard. The couple were picked up as the ship came in to dock at Montreal.

The two fugitives were escorted back to England where Dr Crippen was charged with the murder of his wife and Ethel le Neve with being an accessory after the fact.

When Crippen's trial opened, on October 18th, 1910, it was a media sensation. Over 5,000 applications were received for seats and, despite the bad weather, the crowds piled up outside.

For five days, evidence came before the court to demonstrate the doctor's guilt. The pathologist's report confirmed that the corpse in his cellar had been killed with hyoscine, and it was shown that Dr Crippen had purchased five grains of the poison just prior to the disappearance of his wife. More intriguingly, the prosecution also displayed a thin sliver of skin, four inches in length and approximately a quarter of an inch wide, which displayed an old surgical scar. It was this, they claimed, which proved that the remains found in the cellar were those of Belle Elmore. The police related their whole story.

Crippen had his defenders. Many people described him as a courteous, pleasant and unselfish man. One witness described him as the nicest man she had ever met. Few believed him capable of murder. Their testimony, however, did Crippen little good. The jury returned a verdict of guilty and the sentence of death was passed.

As he waited for his execution, Harvey Crippen wrote a letter to Ethel le Neve. It was a moving farewell:

"Death has no terror for me..but Oh! wifie, my love, my own, the bitterness of the thought that I must leave you alone without me in the world..."

On November 23rd, 1910, at Pentonville Prison, Dr Hawley Harvey Crippen walked calmly to the scaffold. In compliance with his last request, Ethel's photograph and letters were buried with him.

Ethel le Neve was subsequently acquitted of any complicity in the murder of Cora Crippen. Shortly after the trial she emigrated to Canada.

14

STIFLED BY THE STENCH
OF BOILING FLESH

At 11.00 p.m. on July 20th, 1893, nine-year-old Thomas Carter and his young brother were woken up by the row going on downstairs between his father and Rhoda, their new stepmother. The boys scampered to the door to hear more of what was going on. The couple had quarrelled very little since Rhoda had come to live with them a few months ago. But that night there were sounds of screams and shouts and blows. Then they heard Rhoda cry: "No John, no! The Lord have mercy on me."

After that there was silence. Peace was restored and the little boys went back to sleep.

The following morning everything was normal. Rhoda Carter seemed not to be around but the boys were roused as usual by their father at half-past four and marched downstairs. They ate their breakfast and set about their chore of herding the cows just the same as every other day. The boys lingered on their way, watching their father work. He was taking some firewood out to the smithy which separated the cottage from the stables and barn. He also took out the large cauldron.

Rhoda's mother, Mrs Titcombe, lived less than 50 yards away and she used to drop in to see her daughter most mornings. John didn't much care for this as it interrupted Rhoda's household duties, but there was little he could do about it.

True to form, at 9 a.m., Mrs Titcombe knocked on the door, but this time she got no reply. She looked through the window and could see Rhoda's green coat hanging on the back of the kitchen door. So she knocked again. At that moment, Carter came out of the smithy.

"Where is Rhoda?" enquired Mrs Titcombe.

"Gone to see her sister at Eastleech," said Carter, quickly.

"Oh, she didn't say anything to me. Is everything all right. John? Is there anything I can do, make the beds or clear away the breakfast things?"

"Beds are already done," he answered curtly, "and the boys will do the breakfast things when they get home."

"How long will Rhoda be away?" Mrs Titcombe asked.

"Didn't say. A day or two, maybe," replied Carter grumpily. "Now, I've got work to do."

With that he disappeared into the smithy again, clanging the doors shut.

That afternoon, after the boys had gone off to school, taking their bread and cheese with them, Anne Butler, who lived just a few doors away from the Carter farm, was hanging up some clothes to dry in her garden. As she was pegging them to the line, she noticed a column of thick, black smoke coming out from the smithy chimney. Annoyed, she took down the wet washing and carried it back inside.

By 3 o'clock the stench that accompanied the smoke had invaded every home in the neighbourhood. It was a terrible smell, sickly and pungent, and it resulted in more than one complaint. Anne Butler vowed that when she next caught sight of Rhoda she'd give her a piece of her mind. But she never did see Rhoda again and neither did anyone else.

Two days passed, then three and still there was no sign of Mrs Carter. Her sister was contacted, but she said that Rhoda had never been there. No one else had any idea where she might be. As expected, the police were summoned and John Carter was questioned.

"I do not know where my wife is. I only wish I did," he

sighed. "I spent yesterday at Eastleech, Highworth and Letchlade looking for her, but none of her relatives could give me a clue. I do believe she has left me."

It was difficult to believe him. What sort of woman would run off leaving her best coat behind? Yet, whilst there were suspicions, there was nothing anyone could do.

On July 25th, however, the truth came out. John Carter walked into the local pub and, over a brief drink with his brother, said shortly, "I must confess something to you. I have killed my wife." With that, he turned his back and left, leaving his brother with a terrible choice to make.

All night long he wrestled with his conscience. By the morning, however, his mind was made up. He walked down to Wantage police station and gave them the terrible news.

John Carter was quickly arrested and his boys put into the care of Mrs Titcombe. Police officers then began a systematic search of the Carter's home. They went from the house to the barn, the stables and then to the smithy.

There, less than three inches below the surface, they found the body of Rhoda Carter, dressed only in a chemise. Her nose had been smashed and her throat badly bruised. There was also plenty of evidence to show that attempts had been made to burn and boil her body.

As the investigation into the crime continued, questions began to arise about Carter's previous wife. She too was supposed to have walked out on him. His old neighbours had been mightily suspicious about the affair. Why would a young woman, devoted to her children, walk out on her five-year-old-son and her baby? But Carter had told the police that he and his wife had had many rows about money and she had often threatened to leave. Furthermore, now that she was gone, he said, he didn't care where she was. Since no corpse had ever been found, there was little more that the police could do.

Now, in the light of Rhoda's death, the investigation was re-opened. People who had known John Carter at his old home were questioned thoroughly and their suspicions were voiced once more. One neighbour recalled the terrible rows Carter had with his wife and said she was convinced that he had "done her in." She suggested that the police excavate an area known as Burnt Leaze, which had been one of Carter's favourite walking places and a place where a body could be easily hidden. The police took her up on her suggestion.

Officers spent days digging the site, but no human remains were discovered there. They broadened their search, and still found nothing.

In the meantime, John Carter was in court and pleading not guilty to Rhoda's murder. It was a pointless plea. There was far too much evidence against him. Even Carter must have recognised the futility of his claim to innocence because halfway through the case he changed his plea. Now he said he was guilty but it had been a terrible accident. He had killed Rhoda in a sudden fit of temper and had then panicked and tried to conceal her body.

The court was not impressed with this new version, however, and refused to consider the reduced charge of manslaughter. The murder charge remained, and it took the jury only a few minutes to decide his guilt. John Carter was thus sentenced to death.

He was hanged at Reading Gaol on December 3rd, 1893. Some time later the body of the other Mrs Carter was discovered. It had been buried less than 50 yards away from their old home.

15

THE IRON MAN OF HULL

Weeks of rumour were confirmed. The murdering fisherman had been released. No one could believe it. He should have been behind bars for the rest of his natural life. That was what the judge had ordered. After all, Bill Burkitt had already killed three times. Yet now he was out again.

Burkitt committed his first murder on August 27th, 1915, when, aged 29, he stabbed his 32-year-old mistress, Mary Tyler, in the throat. It was a callous murder, made more callous still by the way he broke the news to the woman's children: "George," he shouted, when he met one of her sons playing out in the street, "take this key and take the first policeman you meet to your house. You will find your mother dead."

Burkitt never made any attempt to deny responsibility for the killing, but he insisted that he had been provoked. Mary Tyler, he complained, used to nag him. Nagging, the judge pointed out, was not a justification for violence and "if having a nagging wife were to reduce a charge of murder to manslaughter, it would be a dangerous thing." The judge's sound comments, however, failed to impress the jury. They chose to take a more sympathetic view and decided that the charge should indeed be reduced. Burkitt thus avoided the hangman's rope. Instead he was found guilty of manslaughter and sentenced to 12 years' penal servitude.

Nine years later, Burkitt was released and immediately took up with another married but separated woman, 34-year-old Helen Spencer of Lester Avenue, Hull. Their affair, however, was not destined to last long.

Working as a fisherman, Burkitt spent many nights away from home and soon his fevered imagination began to tell him that Helen was enjoying other men's company in his absence. He tackled her on the subject as soon as he returned, and she denied it emphatically. But evidently her denial was not enough. With a viciousness that was fast becoming a habit, Burkitt snatched up his knife and lunged at Helen's throat. She was dead within moments.

Burkitt was convinced that this time the authorities would hang him, a prospect which, not unnaturally, he preferred to avoid. In an act of either utter desperation or extreme cunning he thus made an attempt to kill himself. He did not succeed. The police had already been alerted by Helen's screams and, long before Burkitt had breathed his last, they had smashed into his home. Burkitt was taken to Hull Royal Infirmary and treated for gas poisoning. Then, once again, he was back in court.

It is a feature of the British legal system that a prisoner's previous record is not allowed to be made known to the jury in case it should prejudice them. This served Burkett well at his appearance in Leeds Assizes. Assuming him to be a man who had erred only once, and hearing of his suicide attempt, the jury once again took the lenient view. Yet again Burkitt was judged guilty of manslaughter rather than murder. A sentence of ten years was imposed.

At Dartmoor Prison, Burkitt gloried in the notoriety of a man who had twice dodged the gallows. He was so proud of the achievement that he had two tombstones tattooed on his right arm. "You don't see many badges of honour like that," he'd boast, "That means I've croaked two of 'em."

Burkitt would "croak" a third poor victim before his time was up. Released from Dartmoor in 1935, and now rejoicing in the nickname of the Iron Man, it was not long before he was in the dock again. This time Burkitt's victim was 38-year-old Emma Brooks.

Emma, if Burkitt's story is to be believed, got a quirky thrill out of goading him into a fury. For three and a half years they stayed together, fighting, arguing and shouting. But in February 1939 Emma Brooks taunted Burkitt for the last time. In a fit of temper he strangled her.

For the next few days Burkitt stayed in the house, too scared to venture out. Eventually, however, he could stand it no longer. He strode into the street, walked down to the River Humber and jumped in. He was dragged out of its murky waters before any harm came to him and made a return visit to the Royal Infirmary. Whilst there, however, the police had visited his home and discovered Emma's dead body.

For the third time William Burkitt stood trial on a charge of murder and for the third time the jury found him guilty of the lesser charge of manslaughter. This time, however, the judge felt something had to be done. Turning to the prisoner he made his pronouncement: "The jury did not know what you know and what I knew - that this was the third time you have stood in the dock on a charge of murder. Each time it has been the murder of a woman with whom you had been living. Each time the jury have taken a merciful view... I can see in your case not one redeeming feature. You will be kept in penal servitude for the rest of your natural life."

Luck, however, had not run out on Bill Burkitt. Although he was in prison for fifteen years, in 1954 he became, once again, a free man. He was released on licence from the Home Office. It was, they said, an act of mercy. Burkitt was suffering from incurable cancer and the authorities had decided to admit him to a hospital in Hull.

In August 1955 Burkitt disappeared from the hospital. There was widespread alarm as the residents of Hull learnt that, once more, the killer was on the prowl. Burkitt's sister, in particular, was terrified. It was she who had been a major prosecution witness fifteen years before.

Thankfully, however, Burkitt was found before any

harm befell her and he was taken back to hospital, where he died on Christmas Eve, 1956. There were still only two tombstones tattooed on his arm - he died before having the third one done.

16

THE MAN THEY COULDN'T HANG

On a pleasant morning in the summer of 1879 John Lee, the 14-year-old son of a local farmer, strolled down the cliff path that led to the home of Miss Emma Keyse. Opening the gate, he walked around the cottage to the rear, where he found the back door with the small inscription at the side "Tradesmen's Entrance."

He lifted the knocker and rapped. The door opened to reveal the familiar face of his half-sister, Elizabeth Harris.

"You're late!" she snapped.

"Only a few minutes," said the boy.

"Well, you'll have to do better, I can tell you. She's waiting for you. Now, mind your manners and don't drop your cap."

She ushered the boy past Eliza and Jane Neck, the two sisters employed as servants to the house, and knocked on a door that led to the sitting-room.

"Come in," said a reedy voice.

Seconds later the boy, fumbling with his cap, found himself being scrutinised by a pair of sharp eyes. He was asked to close the door.

A short while later John Lee emerged from the room to find his half-sister waiting for him.

"Well?" she demanded.

"She's taken me on. I'm to work here. But I don't think I'm going to like it." So, young John Lee went to work as a handyman for Miss Emma Keyse of Babbacombe, Devon a sweet but frail woman who had once been a maid to Queen Victoria.

John did his job well enough and his employer was quite content. But the boy possessed a spirit for adventure that wouldn't die and few people expected him to stay. And so it proved to be. Barely a year had gone by before he had bid Miss Keyes and Babbacombe goodbye and had set off to seek his fortune.

Whether Lee ever lived his dreams is doubtful, but he certainly changed jobs often enough. His last chosen profession was that of a thief, a craft in which he was decidedly inept. He was arrested almost immediately and sentenced to six months in Exeter Prison.

Not reformed but at least more realistic when his term was up, Lee resolved to write to Miss Keyse and offer his services to her again. The 68-year-old spinster received his letter some time in January 1884 and was surprised by its apparent candour. She was also heartened by his appeal for her to employ him again and, displaying her characteristic generosity of spirit, she readily agreed.

On his return, John Lee was informed that, being now that much older, he was to assume the functions of butler and footman as well as handyman. His domain was to be the small room politely termed the pantry. He would live there and eat there and also, at night, sleep there on a truckle bed. John observed that his living quarters provided almost as cramped an existence as he had in his Exeter cell, but he accepted it gladly.

Spring turned to summer and autumn soon approached. Lee tried valiantly to be a good servant. He even attempted to treasure the two shillings and sixpence that he received as his weekly wage. His life, after all, was not too bad especially as he had found himself a girl, a lass from Torbay. She seemed enchanted by him. They had even got engaged. Soon they would be wed. Alas, however, when the girl discovered the reality of her fiancé's poverty and lack of prospects, their romance came to a sudden end.

Brought face to face with the cold reality that he had no future before him, that he could not even afford a wife, John Lee became a changed man. He quickly learned to hate his low-paid job and felt no better about the woman who employed him.

Miss Keyse noticed the change in Lee and decided to speak to him about it. She called him into her room.

"John," she said, "I think you would be happier working elsewhere. A young man like you might consider working in the colonies. Getting away overseas where you could make a new life and find scope for your energies."

It was meant kindly, but John Lee didn't take it that way. He felt that his employer was being unfair, a feeling that was enhanced when his pay was reduced by sixpence after a guitar disappeared from the house. "It isn't fair," he complained. "What does the old woman expect?"

It was in the early hours of Saturday morning, November 15th, 1884, that Elizabeth Harris was woken from her slumbers by the strong smell of smoke. Thoroughly alarmed, she crossed to the door and threw it wide. The landing was full of smoke. Still in her bare feet, Elizabeth ran to the room shared by Eliza and Jane. She pounded on the door.

"Fire!" she cried.

The sisters woke immediately and jumped out of bed. It was Eliza who acted most promptly. She threw some clothes over herself and went hurrying downstairs, forcing her way through the dense black smoke that was now filling the house. She pushed her way down the hall and into the dining-room. Then she screamed.

On the floor was the body of Miss Keyse, her head battered and her throat slashed through. Blood from the wound soaked the old woman's clothing and congealed in her hair. It was a disgusting sight.

John Lee was soon proved to be the culprit. Tried and found guilty of what the judge called "as cruel and barbarous a murder as was ever committed," he was sentenced to death. His execution was scheduled for 8 o'clock on Monday, 23rd February, 1885.

After a weekend of heavy rain, the Monday was dry and cold. The prisoner was put in position beneath the gallows, a hood over his head and a rope round his neck. The hangman pulled the leaver. But the trap remained stuck fast. He pulled again and again, and still the prisoner would not drop.

John Lee was removed from the gallows and asked to stand back. They were tested. Immediately the trap doors opened.

The prisoner was brought out for a second time. Once more, the trap doors remained sealed. A much embarrassed executioner told Lee to stand back yet again. This time he tested his apparatus more thoroughly, and it worked perfectly. Perfectly, that is, until John Lee stood on it for a third time.

The prison surgeon, there to pronounce a legal death, begged him to have this terrible farce stopped and eventually it was agreed that Lee should go back to his cell.

"I'm hungry," he told an amazed warder when they returned.

Told of this, the hangman said: "Well, I can't touch any breakfast, so give him mine."

Everybody was astounded by what had happened. The only person who was not surprised was Lee himself, for he dreamed that he would not hang, "God will never permit me to be executed," he had said. And, indeed, He did not. John Lee's sentence was commuted to imprisonment.

17

THE UNUSUAL ANTICS OF
CHARLES MORTIMER

Charles Arthur Mortimer, a 27-year-old lance corporal, was driving through the Hampshire countryside when he came to one of those rather difficult bends in the road. In front of him was Mrs Alice Series, riding her bicycle. Arthur turned the wheel too hard, the car swerved and, as a result, the poor woman was forced off the road and into a ditch.

Mortimer pulled up a few yards further on and put the car into reverse. Winding down the window, he offered his apologies to the casualty. "Terribly sorry," he said, "trouble with the steering."

Alice Series clambered to her feet and came over to the car. Arthur got out to meet her. He gave her a welcoming smile and then, before she could speak, he landed her a thump in the mouth. The poor woman careered backwards, her mouth full of blood. Mortimer hit her again. Even when she was on the ground he continued to beat her.

A little later in the day and a few miles further on, another female cyclist had the misfortune to encounter Mr Mortimer. Just like the unfortunate Mrs Series, Nellie Boyes was also forced off the road. Unlike his previous victim, however, Nellie was not easily intimidated. She raged at the careless driver and showed him her fist. She told him she would contact the police. Mortimer sensed he might have met his match. He started the engine and drove off smartly. Not smartly enough, however, for Miss Boyes had time to note his licence plate number. It turned out to be a stolen car and was found abandoned later that afternoon.

The next day, August 8th, Mortimer was again up to his old tricks, this time in a another stolen automobile. Driving across the railway bridge at Winchfield in Hampshire he collided with 20-year-old Phyllis Oakes. Cycling just ahead of her was her sister Betty, who heard the crash and turned around. She was horrified to see her sister bouncing off the bonnet of Mortimer's car. So too was a sign writer who witnessed the whole affair. He made a note of the licence plate: AGJ 825.

That afternoon, Mortimer, still in the same car, crashed once again into a lady cyclist. Mrs Lilian Rose Harwood was cycling at Crastock, near Knaphill when Mortimer's car bore down on her. He left her unconscious in the ditch into which she had fallen and then helped himself to her handbag and the money that it contained.

The police caught up with Mortimer on the road to Guildford later that day and gave chase. He careered into a parked van. "I have had a drink or two last week," he explained, as the officers placed him under arrest.

Mortimer was charged with grievous bodily harm against both Phyllis Oakes and Lilian Rose Harwood, a charge that was quickly changed to murder when the unfortunate Miss Oakes succumbed to her injuries and died.

Three months later, in November 1935, Charles Arthur Mortimer, was brought to trial at the Winchester Assizes. He maintained it was all an accident but, after three days of hearing of his antics with women on bicycles, the jury disagreed. He was found guilty and sentenced to die.

On January 22nd, however, following a medical inquiry which found him to be clearly insane, his sentence was commuted to life in prison.

18

POETIC MURDER

It was at about 4 o'clock on the afternoon of August 8th, 1951, when the switchboard operator of the News of the World received a call from a public phone-box in Nottingham.

"I want to speak to someone about a murder," the voice announced.

"Just a moment," said the switchboard operator,

A short while later the call was transferred to Norman Rae, the newspaper's crime reporter.

"Hallo," said Rae, "I hear you want to talk about a murder. Which murder are you referring to?"

The voice in Nottingham had a surprise to deliver: "One the police don't know about yet. A woman has been strangled in Sherwood Vale."

The crime reporter sat a little stunned at this. It might be a hoax, but there was something about the caller's voice that was too eager to suggest a hoax. Norman Rae was very experienced. He had interviewed a good many criminals, and knew how some people thought of newspapers as open-handed purchasers of news-scraps. The lure of easy money attracted both the genuine and the phoney. Especially the phoney. He was understandably cautious. "We might be interested," he said.

Herbert Leonard Mills, the author of this extraordinary call, was a 19-year-old Nottinghamshire lad. He claimed he had stumbled across the body whilst he was out walking. Rather than call the police, however, he had called the newspaper. An aspiring poet, he saw it as an ideal opportunity to get his name into print.

He told Rae that he was prepared to give the News of the World the exclusive story. He even had a price in mind: "£250 is what I am asking."

It was an outrageous proposal, but Rae quickly gathered his wits.

"It sounds a good idea," he said, "but it will have to get the editor's approval. Can you call me back in half an hour?"

Mills agreed to call again.

In the thirty minutes that followed Norman Rae spoke to his editor. But he also spoke to the police who were ready to trace the call when Mills phoned back.

When the call came, Rae told Mills that his editor had agreed to the idea in principle but they would need more details before going ahead. Mills readily told the reporter his whole story. He said he had been strolling in a lonely spot in Sherwood Vale, a place he often visited when he wrote his poems, and had seen a bead necklace lying on the ground. He had bent down to pick it up and, out of the corner of his eye, he saw the body of a woman. "Very white and pale it looked," he said, "seemingly dead. I was startled, wondering what I should do. I felt a little unnerved and decided to leave. On the way home, I sat on the bank to think. I sat there and read Shelley's *Ode to Death*. Then I thought of calling the newspaper."

Norman Rae tried to sound as enthusiastic as possible. about the story and began suggesting the sort of themes that Mills's article might explore and the length it might run. Before he could finish giving his ideas however, the line went dead. The police had apprehended his informer.

Now in police custody, Mills was questioned and repeated the story that he had just told to Norman Rae. The police were doubtful that the young man was telling the truth, but they felt they had better investigate. As a consequence Mills was escorted back to Sherwood Vale, where he claimed the corpse had lain, and invited to show them the body. Mills led the police officers over a narrow path until they came to a weed-chocked gully some eight feet deep.

"Down there," Herbert Mills pointed.

Young Mills backed away as they descended to examine the body. The face was blackened and bloated, but the marks where the blows had been struck could still be seen.

A coroner was quickly summoned.

The police were not impressed by the behaviour of Herbert Mills but there seemed nothing to connect him with the actual crime itself. After a prolonged interview and a reprimand, he was allowed to go. Then the police got on with the business of solving the murder.

The victim was identified as a Mrs Mabel Tattershaw, a 48-year-old mother of two. She had disappeared a week before, following a visit to the local cinema. There, a witness said, she got into a conversation with a man seated next to her.

The description of the man was vague and not terribly helpful. But then a forensic study of the corpse's clothing gave the police a further lead. Three human hairs were found on the woman's coat. Furthermore, some fibres from a man's coat were discovered under her fingernails. It would not be an easy case to solve, they reasoned, but the police were now confident they would eventually get their man.

Detective Superintendent Percy Ellington, head of Nottingham C.I.D., began to plan the next stage of the investigation and started to review the evidence that had already been built up. It was then he realised that some things just didn't add up. Getting on the phone to Norman Rae, he summoned the reporter up to Nottingham.

Rae arrived later that day and the two were soon discussing the case.

Ellington began by mentioning the bead necklace that Mills said he had seen.

"Didn't it strike you as strange," the police officer asked, "that the clasp of the necklace was closed, according to Mills, when he picked it up at the scene of the crime?"

"Very strange," Rae admitted, "I hardly knew what to make of it."

"It's also queer," Ellington went on, "that, whilst it was first believed that Mrs Tattershaw had been bludgeoned to death, the fact is that she was strangled. Yet when Mills first phoned you in London, did he not say, 'I've found the body of a strangled woman'? How do you suppose he knew that then?"

"I see what you mean," Rae nodded.

"Moreover," Ellington added, "when he said that it was the white of her face in the thick weeds that caught his eye. But her face was swollen and black from decomposition."

"What all this adds up to," the detective concluded, "is that our young Mr Mills knows considerably more about the crime than he has told us."

A few days later Rae and Mills were together in a hotel room. The two men talked for a couple of hours. Ostensibly they were their to discuss the article that Mills was going to write for the newspaper, but their conversation ranged far more widely. It drifted from horse racing to the legends of Nottingham, from the poetry of Keats to the crime writers of America. Eventually, however, they returned to the matter in hand and the various intricacies of the Tattershaw killing. Rae said that at first he thought it was a perfect crime but then, as always, the criminal's errors had shown up. It was then, just as he appeared on the verge of saying something else, that Mills blurted out his admission: "That was it. I tried to commit the perfect crime of murder. I failed. I want to get it off my chest."

Rae placed some notepaper on a desk and handed the young man a pen. "Go ahead," he said to him, "put it all down."

Mills then made a detailed confession of the murder of Mabel Tattershaw.

He said that on the night of August 2nd, he was in the Roxy cinema when Mrs Tattershaw and another woman came in. They sat down, Mrs Tattershaw next to him.

"She endeavoured to make conversation," he wrote, "Not wishing to be impolite, I answered, trying hard to make it clear that I did not wish it. She invited me to see her the following day. I refused. But she still insisted.

"I am very interested in crime and had always considered the possibility of the perfect murder. Here was my opportunity. So I consented to see her. I met her the following day Friday, August 3rd."

Mills then went on to say that he and Mrs Tattershaw walked out to the lonely woodland, and she lay down on a grassy bank. He asked to examine her necklace and she removed it and gave it to him. He refastened the clasp and dropped the beads into his pocket. Then he seized the woman by the throat and strangled her. He rolled her body down the gully then returned to his grandparents' home.

The young poet admitted to Rae that his confession was prompted by the growing fear that detectives were close on his trail and might arrest him at any moment.

His learning that they had found hairs from his head and fibres from his blue pin-stripe suit which Ellington had seen him wear were the things which finally drove him to make his statement.

"I was almost successful. No motive, no clue. If I had not reported the finding of the body, I should not have been connected with the murder in any manner whatsoever. I am quite proud of my achievement."

Mills signed the confession and then accompanied Rae to police headquarters where the newspaperman delivered the five-page document. Herbert Mills was subsequently charged with murder.

At his trial the would-be poet showed scant remorse. Instead, for most of the time he appeared very smug. "The strangling itself was quiet easily accomplished," he said at one point, "I was very pleased. I think I did it very well."

Not well enough, however.

On November 23rd, 1951 Herbert Leonard Mills was found guilty and sentenced to death. He was hanged at Lincoln Prison on December 11th.

19

DEATH AMONG THE BLUEBELLS

While idling away a twilight evening on a quiet beach at Barry, Glamorgan, Joseph Christopher Reynolds, a 23-year-old Irish labourer, saw a young woman walking slowly along the tranquil beach. He fell into step beside her, chatting. She, however, didn't care for his company. Feeling threatened and uneasy, she told him to go about his business. She even offered him money, hoping he would take it and be gone.

Reynolds declined the woman's offer. Instead he pulled out a large knife that had been hidden in his clothing and brandished it before her.

The woman screamed in terror as Reynolds lunged forward. He stabbed at her, plunging the knife into her chest and back. Then he punched her, shouting out his inner rage. "I am going to kill you!" he yelled.

Shocked by the sight of her own blood, the woman made a desperate attempt to repel her attacker. She kicked, punched, clawed and bit with every savage instinct she could summon. Stunned by one of her blows, Reynolds fell to the ground, but quickly scrambled back to his feet. Instead of returning to the fight, however, he turned tail. Within moments he had disappeared across the sands.

The woman, badly wounded and covered in blood, staggered home and summoned the police. The alert went out that a maniac with a knife was on the loose.

Reynolds was found quite easily and promptly charged with attempted murder, Reynolds made no attempt to deny the crime. He didn't know the woman and had no grievance against her, but he had indeed tried to kill her. He tried to explain his perverse motives to the officers: "I have been depressed for a week and didn't want to live. I thought that if I murdered her, I would be hanged and die that way."

A few months later Reynolds offered the same explanation to twelve puzzled jurors at the Cardiff Assize Court. They had no hesitation in finding him guilty. Joseph Christopher Reynolds was sentenced to three years' imprisonment.

Eight years later, on the evening of May 22nd, 1953, at Blaby, Leicestershire, Reynolds was free again and his sojourn behind bars had clearly done nothing to assuage his desire to kill. In fact it was now stronger than ever.

Lurking on a canal towpath, a woman's stocking in his hands, Reynolds waited for a victim. He'd been beset by evil thoughts for days and had been visiting the towpath for more than a week. So far no one suitable had crossed his path. But today was different. Today was the day he would strike.

Twelve-year-old Janet Warner skipped happily along the towpath, her black-and-white mongrel dog running on ahead. Just off the towpath, Janet wandered into the spinney known as Blue Banks Wood and, unaware that she was being hungrily watched by the murderous ex-convict, stooped down and began to gather some bluebells.

She picked a small bunch and lay them next to a stone. She then returned to the patch of flowers and selected a few more. There was a whole carpet of them under the trees and she was spoilt for choice.

Two local boys were also in the spinney that day, but they paid no attention to little Janet. They were climbing a tree, searching for birds' eggs, and with that intense concentration peculiar to boys outside the classroom, they noticed nothing else. Janet's dog ran up to their tree and that distracted them for a second, but, soon enough, they were again engrossed in their work.

But then they heard another noise which they couldn't ignore. There was a crash followed by a strangled cry.

The boys scrambled down from the tree to investigate. From a hiding place behind the bushes, and hidden by the undergrowth, they spied a man kneeling on the ground. He had a strap wrapped around a little girl's neck and was choking her. Horrified, the boys raced off to find a policeman.

After the pitiful body of young Janet Warner had been located by the police, a massive manhunt for the killer was set in motion. Villagers joined forces with police and soldiers as they combed the area with tracker dogs.

Road-blocks were set up, police mounted a watch on all ports and even an Army Auster spotter plane was brought in for the search. But Reynolds evaded them all. The boys had given a good discription of the man. The police soon knew who it was that they were after. But it seemed that the man had disappeared off the face of the earth.

Two days later, however, on Sunday, a sharp-eyed policeman caught sight of Reynolds in Leicester's city centre. He gave chase and was led on a merry run through the city's almost deserted streets before cornering the murderer in an alleyway. Reynolds was overpowered. Then he was arrested and duly charged with Janet Warner's murder.

Reynolds readily confessed to the killing, expressing concern about whether the child's dog had returned home safely. He then was taken to a cell where he spoke no more.

At Leicester Assizes, Reynolds' case lasted only four minutes - one of the briefest murder trials in criminal annals. The prisoner made only one statement: "I have nothing to say, my Lord, I deserve the extreme punishment for my crime. I am heartily sorry for the little girl and the grief I cause her parents. I am happy to die."

Joseph Christopher Reynolds finally achieved his wish. A few days later, on a summer's morning in 1953, he was led to the gallows and to death.

20

BLOOD ON THE CARPET

At 8.45 on the morning of February 18th, 1936, James Rafferty was finishing his paper round when he cast his eyes towards the sea and noticed a car jammed in the barrier at the end of Corbawn Lane in the village of Shankhill, County Dublin. Judging by the way the vehicle was wedged, the driver had tried to ram his way through the opening and got stuck.

Rafferty could see that the driver's door had been left open, as had the sunroof. Musing over the stupidity of some car owners, he scrambled down the lane to investigate. But, when he was close enough to see inside the car he froze with horror.

The dashboard, the steering wheel and the lower part of the windscreen were thickly smeared with blood. There was also blood on the seats and a blood saturated towel draped over the back seat. Rafferty had got more than half-way to the Garda barracks before he realised he was running.

It took six police officers to dislodge the two-door Austin from the grip of the barrier. They had to be careful not to trample the bloodstained ground or kick the blood splashed tyres as they worked.

Documents inside the glove compartment revealed that the owner of the car was Mrs Lavinia Ball, the 55-year-old wife of a well-known Dublin doctor. A pair of officers were dispatched to her house, 23 St. Helen's Road, Booterstown, Dublin, to interview her.

The Ball household was evidently reasonably affluent. The house was a detached one, well furnished and had a garage. As the officers arrived, the maid, Lily Kelly, was laying the table in preparation for a dinner party later that evening. She told them that Mrs Ball was out for the time being, but she would be willing to fill them in with background information about the family herself.

Mrs Ball, Lily explained, had been living apart from her husband since 1927, but one of her two sons, 20- year-old Edward, had recently moved back in with her.

The police returned to the house that evening and found Edward Ball alone at home. A pleasant, intelligent young man, he showed no surprise that they were asking about his mother's whereabouts. He had last seen her at 7.45 the previous evening, driving away in her car. She'd told him she would be staying the night with some friends, maybe her sister, and seemed perfectly cheerful when he closed the drive gates after her.

Edward's father had already told him that his mother's car had been founded damaged at Shankhill, with blood-stains inside and the boy was intrigued. When the police elaborated on the incident and mentioned the blood soaked towel he could contain his curiosity no longer: "I wonder whether there would be more blood on it than if a person had cut their hand or by an accident?"

Edward was asked about his relationship with his mother. He said that they had recently had a row. The previous evening he had clumsily broken a cup from a rather valuable tea-set and she had shouted at him, but the incident was soon over. When asked about his own background, Edward explained that he had been obliged to give up his Dublin flat because, on the allowance he was given, he couldn't afford the rent. That was why he had moved in with his mother of February 13th, despite the fact he wasn't especially welcome. She'd actually complained, in the presence of Lily, of how unfortunate it was that she had responsibility for him until he was 21.

It was shortly after this that detectives began to search the house. In Edward's room they found a pair of shoes, sodden and covered in mud, and a newspaper parcel containing wet and bloodstained linen. They then tried to get access into his mother's bedroom. The door was locked, but the boy cheerfully agreed to let the police force open the door.

The room was in darkness, the curtains drawn, but an electric fire was blazing away, in an obvious attempt to dry a large wet stain on the carpet.

It was now time to begin a more thorough search. Forensic experts were brought in. They discovered traces of blood all over the house. There was blood on the landing, the stairs and in the kitchen. More than 19 items in Mrs Ball's bedroom were also bloodstained, including the bed-head, mattress, dressing table, bedside lamp, hot water bottle and hand basin. There was also blood in Edward's room.

Outside there was blood on the path, on the garage floor and a bloodstained hatchet in the garden shed. They also discovered a suitcase that Edward had left at the flat of one of his friends. It contained women's clothing and bed-linen, all heavily soaked with blood.

Faced with what the police had found, Edward Ball confessed knowledge of his mother's death. He sadly explained that he had found her lying dead on her bed, having cut her own throat with a razor blade. His attempts to cover it up, he said, were solely to protect her reputation. He went on to admit that he dragged her corpse down to the sea and let the tide carry it away.

Although Mrs Ball's body was never recovered, Edward's suicide story was not believed. Pathologist Dr John McGrath said that suicide was not a likely cause of death because the woman's hair had been found on the hatchet blade. If she had killed herself, she would have lifted her hair out of the way. Moreover, it was demonstrated that over four pints of her blood had spilled on bedroom carpet, which conflicted with the notion that she cut her throat on the bed. Edward Ball was thus duly charged with matricide.

At his trial, which began on February 21st, 1936, great play was made of his mother's mental instability. Edward's father testified that Lavinia Ball did have suicidal tendencies and two members of her family had already died by their own hand. She was a kleptomaniac as well, and also a depressive. Her depressions, he said, often last weeks, during which time she would speak to no one. It was the strain of these, he declared, that caused him to leave her nine years earlier. And she had not got any better. Just two months before her death, Mrs Ball had been in hospital suffering from nervous debility.

In the face of all the forensic evidence, however, the jury was unconvinced. Neither was Edward Ball's case helped when the questions about mental health were also directed at him. He too, it transpired, was severely disturbed.

In the absence of a body, the jury was faced with a difficult decision. It took more than five hours to reach a verdict. They judged Edward Ball guilty, but insane.

21

THE SAUSAGE MAKER

Adolf Luetgert emigrated to America from his native Germany in the 1870s and within three years he had earned the reputation of making the best German sausages in Chicago. Customers flocked to buy his products. They were popular with everyone, not only the sizeable German immigrant population, but also other citizens of various nationalities and ethnic origins who enjoyed good food.

Adolf Luetgert enjoyed food himself, perhaps a little too much. He tipped the scales at a hefty 250 pounds, or close to 18 stones. Yet, vast though his gastronomic appetite was, it was paltry when compared to his tremendous appetite for sex. He had no fewer than three regular mistresses, as well as his wife. Moreover, he had a bed installed in his office at the factory and here his typists, secretaries and factory workwomen were also invited to enjoy his company.

Adolf Luetgert was happy and contented with this set-up except for one thing: his wife. "She annoys me," he told one mistress. "I could take her and crush her!" he complained to another. To a third he declared that sex with his wife was "like trying to flog a dead horse."

One evening in late April 1897, Louisa Luetgert left their home to make a visit to her mother's. Adolf was pleased to let her go. He said the longer she was away for, the better he would feel. But when, after some days, Louisa had still not returned and then her mother turned up at the factory demanding to know where she was, Adolf Luetgert started to panic.

"I understood she was staying with you," he said. "She told me she was going out to see you and, when she did not come back, I naturally assumed she was still there."

"She has not visited me at all," the woman declared.

"Then where can she be?" asked Adolf.

"That's what I'm asking you," screeched her mother, "You know it's not like her to go anywhere without telling either you or me. Something must have happened to her. We should report this to the police."

"Oh no!" cried Adolf, "As a prominent businessman in this city, I could not possibly afford a scandal. My business would be ruined!"

"Why?" the woman asked, "do you think she has run off with another man?"

"I shouldn't think so," pondered Adolf, "but you never can tell with women.

"I'll tell you what I'll do," he went on, "I'll hire a private detective to find her. They're very good, you know. Nine times out of ten they find the person they're looking for."

The mother of Louisa Luetgert had to be content with this for the time being. But, after a few days had passed and there was still no news of the missing woman, she thought that enough was enough and decided to inform the police herself. On May 1st, 1897, and without Luetgert's knowledge, Louisa's disappearance was officially reported.

When a wife is missing, the husband is always the first suspect. Thus the police gave Adolf a hard time, interrogating him at length and questioning his every move. But he stuck to his story that she had gone out, saying she was going to visit her mother. He insisted that he had no idea where she was. He admitted that he never actually hired any private detectives, though he had intended to. He gave the police the distinct impression that he was far more concerned with the effect of a scandal on his business than with the whereabouts of his wife.

The police could see they were getting nowhere merely

asking questions so they now decided to search his entire factory. They went from top to bottom, searching every nook and corner. Asked why he kept a bed in his office, Adolf explained that it was for him to sleep on when he had to work late. It was hardly worthwhile going home in the early hours when he had to be back at work at 7 a.m.

The police found nothing in the building, but then they decided to empty Adolf's steam vats and search the sludge at the bottom. The first three vats produced nothing untoward, but the fourth one confirmed the suspicions they had all secretly shared. In the sludge at the bottom they found fragments of human bone, human teeth and two gold wedding rings, one of which was engraved with the initials L.L.

Louisa Luetgert's mother and several other relatives identified both rings as having belonged to the missing woman and, as a consequence, the sausage maker was taken into custody and charged with the murder of his wife.

Luetgert strongly denied the charge, insisting that he knew nothing of his wife's whereabouts. He denied that the bone fragments could be human, pointing out that pig meat was used in the manufacture of his sausages and that, anatomically, pig's bones are very similar to human's. The teeth, he declared, could be false teeth, which one of his factory workers had perhaps let fall into the vat during cleaning operations. The rings were certainly not his wife's, he said. His wife had suffered from swollen, arthritic finger-joints and had been unable to remove either of her rings for years.

The police then pointed out that one ring bore his wife's initials.

"Don't be stupid!" raged Luetgert. "My wife is not the only woman with the initials L.L. There must be hundreds, maybe even thousands, of women with the same initials in Chicago!"

"Yes," replied his interrogator, "but isn't it unlikely that one of those other women dropped their rings in your vat?"

The trial of Adolf Luetgert was sensational. Nothing like

it had ever happened in Chicago before. Every day, hordes of people thronged the streets outside the court, which was crowded to capacity.

One mistress after another went on the witness-stand to testify against Adolf. They were followed by a long procession of typists, secretaries and factory workwomen who had been gullible enough to fall for the plausible blandishments of the tubby Don Juan. Not one of them could recall a kind word that Adolf had said about his wife.

Adolf Luetgert still denied all knowledge of the crime, but his protestations came to nothing. He was convicted of murder in the first degree.

Sentenced to life imprisonment, he died in Joliet prison in 1911.

For years afterwards his crime was still remembered. Even today you occasionally here the chant of Chicago's children:

Adolf was a dirty rat,
He boiled his wife for sausage fat.

22

HIS SPELLING WAS HIS DOWNFALL

"Lady cook, 31, requires post in school. Experience in school with 40 boarders. Disengaged. Salary £65. Miss Irene Wilkins, 21 Thirlmere Road, Streatham, S.W.16." So appeared the advertisement in the Morning Post of December 22nd, 1921. And it worked surprisingly well. Before midday, a telegram boy was knocking at the door of no. 21 to deliver a buff coloured envelope.

"For Miss Irene Wilkins," he announced.

A few seconds later, Irene Wilkins called out to her mother and sister.

"Look," she said, "It's a reply. They want me at once. Isn't it wonderful? Just like a Christmas present."

She displayed the telegram proudly, for all to see:

"Morning Post. Come quickly 4.30 train Waterloo. Bournmouth Central. Car will meet train. Expence no object. Urgent. Wood, Beech House"

Irene hurried about the house, gathering a few clothes and belongings and packing them into a case for the trip. Within a few hours she was ready. She travelled from Waterloo the same afternoon, exactly as instructed, and arrived at Bournemouth Central Station at about 7 p.m. But, alas, she soon discovered that the telegram was not all that it seemed. With its bad spelling and fictitious address, it was not drawing her to employment. It was luring her to her death.

Early next morning Irene Wilkins' mutilated body was found on waste ground between Bournemouth and Christchurch. She had died of haemorrhage and shock resulting from savage wounds to her head and brain.

A copy of the decoy telegram was flashed on the screen of every cinema in the town, in the hope that somebody would be able to recognise the handwriting. Nobody came forward.

Post Office officials were vague in their memory of the person who had handed the telegram in, but one clerk was sure that it had been a chauffeur, "a man," she said, "with a rough voice."

People who had been at Bournemouth Central Station at the time Irene had arrived were appealed to for any recollection they might have of the girl herself, or of anyone meeting her there. A dozen or so came forward but their information was of little use. Then Frank Humphries, an engineer from Boscombe, appeared. He said he had been on the same train as the girl and had seen her being driven away. He knew the make of the car, a Mercedes. He even knew its licence plate number, LX 7405. This should have been the breakthrough in the case, but it wasn't. In one of those foolish errors that happen every now and again in police enquiries, his report was simply filed away.

Weeks went by, then months, and no arrest was made. Soon the Wilkins murder began to look like one of those crimes that would remain forever unsolved. But the police had not given up.

At length, Superintendent Shadrach Garratt, who had been in charge of the case from the beginning, resolved to go once more through all the 22,000 documents which had been accumulated during his investigation. In doing so, Frank Humphries' statement reappeared. Garratt immediately saw its potential significance.

The car turned out to have been owned by one Mr Sutton of Barton Close, Southbourne. His chauffeur was a 36-year-old army deserter by the name of Thomas Henry Allaway.

Allaway's name had already cropped up in the course of their earlier investigations and Inspector Garratt had a strong hunch that he was the man they were after. But what they needed now was a link to be found between the chauffeur and the decoy telegram.

Very quietly the police went to work to secure specimens of his handwriting, but there was little available as Allaway had no occasion to write in the usual run of his life. But then Garratt heard that Allaway was in the habit of writing to a friend in Scotland. He made arrangements to contact him.

Whether the friend told Allaway that the police were making enquiries is not certain. But, almost immediately afterwards, Allaway made preparations to leave. He had no money, so he stole some cheque-forms from his employer. Then he departed from Bournemouth, at the same time sending his wife and seven-year-old daughter to her parent's home in Reading.

Police learnt of his escape and mounted watch on his in-laws home. On the evening of April 28th, Allaway was observed approaching the house, but he recognized the constable standing guard outside and bolted. The police-man gave chase, but his age and weight were against him. Indeed Allaway would have got away had not a passer-by, seeing the chase, stuck out his foot. Allaway went sprawling and, before he could stand up, the policeman reached him, sat on his back and put on the handcuffs.

Back in Bournemouth, Superintendent Garratt now had the difficult task of proving Allaway to be the sender of the telegram. To begin with, witnesses were invited to identi-fication parades to see if they could pick out any person to whom their evidence applied.

The postal clerk picked Allaway out as resembling the man who handed in the telegram. She also recognised his voice. Two others, and a railway signal man, identified him as the man who was at the railway station, with a car, at 7 p.m. on the day of the murder.

At Allaway's lodgings in Boscombe, police discovered a letter and some postcards in his handwriting. Fortune was at last favouring the cause of justice, for these showed Allaway as the probable writer of the decoy telegrams. And, when he agreed to write out, to the dictation of the officers, the text of the telegram, his fate was sealed. Although Allaway made every attempt to disguise his handwriting, he faithfully reproduced his spelling errors. "Bournemouth" was rendered with out an "e," expense was spelt with a "c."

On July 3rd, 1922, Thomas Allaway was put on trial at Winchester Assizes. Four days later the jury returned a verdict of guilty.

As sentence was passed, Allaway was heard gasping. His dark face turned purple as he cried out in a strangled moan: "I am innocent of this crime absolutely."

Allaway lodged an appeal but, though the three judges considered the question of the apparent lack of motive, the appeal was dismissed. Senseless, it may have been, they reasoned. But there was no question over Allaway's guilt.

Allaway continued to protest his innocence to friends and family but, on the night before his execution, he confessed the crime to the prison governor. Even then, however, he could not say why he had done it.

Thomas Henry Allaway was led to the gallows in the early hours of August 19th, 1922. His death, it was said, was not an easy one. Because of a hitch in the operation of the thread of silk which holds the noose in position. he was actually hanged in the ancient manner, dying by strangulation instead of dislocation. The prison doctor was asked at the inquest: "Was death instantaneous?" After a slight hesitation, he replied: "Yes, practically."

23

THE MAN IN PLUS-FOURS

At about 10 a.m. on Friday, October 2nd, 1931 the body of 20-year-old Norah Upchurch was found in an empty shop in Shaftesbury Avenue, London. The girl's corpse lay in a passageway between the front and the rear of the store. Her white silk blouse had been torn and used as a gag. The belt from her skirt had been knotted around her throat. Her green hat, her gloves and a cheap brooch lay nearby.

The last person to have had a key to the building was a certain Frederick Field, a signboard fixer. He had obtained the keys from the estate agents the previous Saturday to take down a "To Let" board. The police were thus very eager to speak to him.

Frederick Field was a personable young man and very keen to help the police with their investigation. He had been as shocked by the murder as anyone and doubtless wanted to see the culprit brought swiftly to justice. But the police were wrong in one respect of their enquiry. Field was not the last person to have had a key to the shop. A gentleman with an "order to view" had collected one from him some days before.

Field explained that, when he was working in the shop, a man had come in with a letter of authority from the estate agency. He said he would be renting the shop for his business and needed to check it over. Field said the man was quite tall, well-built and had a noticeable tan. He wore plus-fours and had a gold tooth. Field did his best to give the police all the detail he could recall. But it did no good. The mysterious stranger in plus-fours was never found.

The case dragged on for month after month and still the police were no closer to making an arrest. And then, in a remarkable turn of events, Frederick Field turned up, once again, at Great Marlborough Street police station. "I want to give myself up for the murder of Norah Upchurch," he declared.

It was July 25th, 1933, nearly two years after the murder, and the police were utterly bewildered by the confession. True, some of them had had their suspicions. But no evidence against Field had been gathered. There was no prospect of his arrest. And yet, here he was, boldly making his confession.

"I lost my temper and gripped her round the throat," he said, "She seemed to faint away and fell back out of my hands on to the floor. She didn't scream or speak. I knew there was something seriously wrong when she fell back, and I lost control of myself. I cannot remember exactly what happened afterwards...

"The reason I have come to the police to give myself up," he went on, "is because I am fed up. My outlook is bad, and through arrangements I have made, my wife and child will be better off without me." Those arrangements, which in the end came to nothing, turned out to be an attempt to sell his story to a newspaper.

Field's confession tied in with the facts and the police believed it was genuine. They thus placed the signboard fixer under arrest and committed him for trial.

But at his trial Field delivered a second surprise. Boldly pleading that he was not guilty he retracted the statement he had made to the police and reverted to his earlier story concerning the man in plus-fours. Asked why he had made the confession, he told the court that, after the inquest on Norah Upchurch, he felt he had no chance of proving his innocence.

"I wanted the whole thing cleared up properly," he said.

"The whole thing was left in the air. People said, 'This man has done it.' I couldn't turn round and say: 'I have been proved innocent.' I couldn't say anything. I wanted to be put on trial, because by doing that I could have my innocence proved properly."

"It is a peculiar way of proving your innocence to say you are guilty," commented Mr Justice Swift.

"It was the only way," Field replied.

The judge then had to tell the jury that the only evidence against Field was his own statement. He was obviously a liar, but they could not convict him of murder because of that. Field was accordingly found not guilty and discharged.

Field's next move was to go to a newspaper, offering to sell his story. He told them that he really had killed Norah Upchurch, and he had got away with it. Having been acquitted, he could not be tried for the crime again.

In a confession, which he wrote for the newspaper, he claimed that Upchurch had been blackmailing him, threatening to reveal to his wife that they were having an affair and to tell his employer that they were using company buildings for their sex-sessions. "Some courts classify blackmail as moral murder," he declared. " She got what she deserved." The newspaper which brought the story decided it was not in the public interest to print it and filed it away. But Field didn't keep silent. He took to bragging about his exploits at every opportunity, ensuring that everyone within earshot knew what a clever fellow he was: the man who had outwitted Scotland Yard and the best legal brains in Britain.

Three years later, another woman was found murdered. She was Mrs Beatrice Vilna Sutton and her body had been found at her home in Edgeley Road, Clapham. Frederick Field was, again, the obvious suspect and he was immediately brought in for questioning.

"Yes," he admitted, "I killed her."

"I knew I was going to murder her. I put my hands around her neck and strangled her. When I was sure she was dead I put a pillow over her face because I didn't want to look at her. I had never seen that woman before in my life, and I killed her just because all of a sudden I wanted to kill somebody."

Field's confession tallied perfectly with the facts of the murder and there was no doubt in anyone's mind that he was the killer. But the police weren't going to be caught out twice. They went over every detail, corroborating it with other evidence, backing it up with other statements and facts. In essence, they pretended that the confession had never been made.

It was a laborious process but one that soon proved worth its while. Appearing at the Old Bailey for his second murder trial, Frederick Field again retracted his confession.

"I did not kill Mrs Sutton," he told the jury, before commencing a long-winded account of overhearing a quarrel, finding her dead body and running from her home as fast as he could.

This time, however, with the extra evidence, Field's ploy failed. The jury all found him guilty and Frederick Field was sentenced to death.

Frederick Field passed his time while awaiting execution by playing chess. He was the best player in Wandsworth Prison. He told his relatives: "The guard who looks after me is my nearest competition, and he owes me a lot of money. I'll probably never be able to spend it, but I'm still hoping."

Despite his predicament, Field still managed to display a wry humour. "If you want to come to visit me, you know my address," he wrote to a friend. "I'm always in." The noose into which he'd talked himself with his second confession finally tightened on June 30th, 1936.

24

THE PROSTITUTE AND THE AIRMAN

In retrospect Ronald True's father must have realised that sending his child abroad had been a mistake. It had been done with the best intentions, of course. Ronald had left school at 17 and was still as lazy and worthless as ever. Travel abroad, thought his father, would make a man of him. But it didn't. It just gave him a taste for fast living and a drug habit.

The outbreak of war provided Ronald True with the excuse to return to England and in 1915 he was enlisted into the Royal Flying Corps. In the art of flying, True showed no more industry or ability than he had displayed in any other area of his life and yet, to the utter amazement of his fellow pilots, he actually passed his flying test and won his wings. Ronnie made a great deal of this success and promptly ordered wings insignia three times larger than normal issue. There was scant cause for celebration, however, when he crashed his plane on his first solo flight nor a month later when he crashed again and, as a consequence, was invalided out of the Flying Corps.

Ronald took this opportunity to travel to New York where he regaled everyone with daring tales of his illustrious flying career. He made grand claims about his rank and his record as a fighter ace, and most people believed him. His reputation soon assured him of a place on everybody's guest list and his life became a social whirl of parties, nightclubs, hotels, tea-rooms and dance halls. He also married Frances Roberts, an actress, and the couple gaily wandered around America, Mexico and Cuba until his father, once again, intervened. He despatched Ronald to a Gold Coast mining company in the hope that his son might, at last, start earning a living.

Inevitably, the plan failed. Inside six months Ronnie had been dismissed and, now a hopeless morphine addict, he returned to England. Efforts were made to help with his drug problem. He was sent to various nursing homes and hospitalised a number of times. But, eventually, his exasperated father washed his hands of him, giving him an allowance but no more help. Then Ronnie's behaviour towards his two-year-old son became unpredictable and dangerous, and his wife gave up on him too. She had him certified insane.

It was in the early part of 1922 that Ronnie decided that there must be another Ronald True who was responsible for all his bad deeds. He told his friends that a man, someone who looked almost exactly like him, had been travelling the country and causing no end of problems. It was this other Ronald True, he said, who was responsible for all the bad debts, the dud cheques and the thefts.

The notion about another Ronald True began as a harmless enough delusion. Soon, however, it had escalated into full-blown paranoia. True even bought himself a gun so he could assassinate the evil doppelgänger.

Shortly afterwards, Ronald True was living it up in lavish splendour at the Grand Hotel in London's Northumberland Avenue. He had acquired a chauffeur-driven car from a hire firm, and was travelling to dances and tea rooms in Richmond and Reading. Then, in the evenings, just before midnight, he would return to London and call upon a certain Olive Young.

Olive Young was a shrewd, high-class prostitute. A clever woman, she had built up a wealthy regular clientele and accrued a considerable amount of money in the bank. She had decided, however, that one of her regulars, "Major

True," would be welcome no more. The last time they had met he had stolen £5 from her purse. This was not how her business was intended to work and she declared that she would not entertain him again.

However, on Sunday March 5th, just after midnight, True appeared once more. Standing outside her Fulham flat, he looked as though he might cause a fuss. As Olive was naturally anxious that he should not create a disturbance, she agreed that he come in. True dismissed his chauffeur and walked through her door.

At some time during the morning, after the milkman and the newspaper man had made their deliveries, Ronnie made a cup of tea for himself and Olive. As she sat up in bed to drink it he struck her five times over the head with a rolling pin, and then calmly drank his tea and ate some biscuits.

At 9.15 a.m. the maid, Miss Steel, arrived and Ronnie, before leaving, told her not to disturb her mistress. He said she was deep in sleep. He tipped the maid very handsomely and left, saying he would send a car for Miss Young at about midday.

It was over an hour before Miss Steel found the body and called for help. Not only had the young woman been bludgeoned, but as subsequent police examination showed, a piece of rough towelling had been thrust into her mouth and a dressing gown cord had been knotted round her neck.

In such circumstances, most murderers would have made every effort to disappear from public view, but True unconcernedly went on a clothes-buying spree. It was as though he was deliberately laying a trail for himself.

He made no attempt to evade the law and the police located him with the minimum of effort that evening. He was arrested in his box at the Hammersmith Palace of Varieties.

True made a brief statement to the police in which he described a man who had been in Miss Young's flat at the time of his arrival. He also said that, after a scene, he had left. But on March 7th he was charged with the wilful murder of Mrs Gertrude Yates (Olive Young's real name) and held for trial at Brixton Prison.

When he appeared at the Old Bailey in May 1922, Ronald True's counsel tried to establish his client's insanity. But, whilst the prosecution agreed that the prisoner might be deranged, they contended that he still knew the difference between right and wrong. The jury chose to agree, and True was found guilty.

Subsequently, however, the Home Secretary had True examined by a board of three psychiatrists, all of whom concluded that he was suffering from a congenital mental disorder, aggravated by drug addiction.

Ronald True avoided the hangman's noose and, instead, was sent to Broadmoor, where, cheerful and popular, he spent the rest of his life.

25

THE ONE-LEGGED KILLER

Twenty-six year old Eugene de Vere had led an eventful life. He came from Renfrew, in Scotland, where he had been apprenticed to a tailor. He then joined the Black Watch and served with the army overseas. A succession of odd jobs followed, and at 18 he became an Air Force cadet, subsequently needing to have his left leg amputated after it became septic due to the rubbing of a heavy boot. He remained in the Air Force as a tailor, leaving the service in 1920. Then de Vere moved to London and began a double life: a beggar by day, a dandy by night.

Hiring a barrel organ, he posed as a wounded officer and begged for money on the streets. Once he got home, however, those who had supported him with their small change would not have known him. Attaching his artificial leg and slipping into a dress suit for which he'd paid 14 guineas, he became a regular man-about-town, cavorting about the city's nightclubs and lingering in the bars.

Eugene had many girlfriends and mistresses, but one in particular had captured his heart. She was 17-year-old Polly Walker, a pretty, golden-haired girl with whom he was utterly besotted.

Polly lived with her widowed mother and her brother, Frank, in a flat in Arlington Road, Camden Town, not far from Eugene's own rooms. The young man had got to know them when, at the beginning of his London career, he was down on his luck and could barely afford his rent, let alone food to eat. Taking pity on him, Polly's mother, who worked as a cinema cleaner, arranged that he should have his meals at her flat each day, Eugene paying her when he could afford to. "He was down and out," Frank said later. "As he had no friends in the world, we were sorry for him and thought we were doing a Christian act in helping him."

At first, Polly did nothing to discourage Eugene's advances and, when he began making some money, she readily flirted with him. But she was irritated by his possessiveness and the way he resented her other male friends. Polly liked to play the field, and when Eugene's continual presence and attention began cramping her style, she complained long and hard.

One person who took an interest in the couple was the Revd W. Jones, curate of St. Mary's, Somers Town. Polly had first taken Eugene to St. Mary's in 1924, and the two became regular church goers.

"He seemed to be very much attracted to the girl," the curate later declared, "And, at first, she was very fond of de Vere. But it did not last long. She told me she was tired of him and wanted to be rid of him. She was very fond of the company of the opposite sex, and liked to be with the boys. I think that her friendship with other men was certainly provocative to de Vere. She did not take him seriously."

It was the curate who first advised Polly to give him up, and she had readily agreed. But she didn't want to say goodbye to him until after Christmas had passed. She didn't want to miss her present.

"I took her to task about that and told her it was not the straight thing to do," said the curate.

But even the curate new that things were not as simple as all that. Earlier in their relationship, de Vere had been driven to such desperation by Polly's refusal to go out with him that he had attempted suicide by taking poison and had been admitted to hospital. Visiting him there, the curate had urged the young man to stay away from the girl. He had also warned her mother of the consequences that might ensue if the relationship were not ended. But it had still lingered on and on.

In December 1925, the Walkers finally decided that they would have to ask de Vere not to come again to their home, and to keep away from Polly. But they put off telling him for a few days. For Frank and Mrs Walker it seemed the kindest thing to do, for Polly it made sense too.

Thus Eugene was invited as usual to the small party that the Walkers held on Christmas Day at their home. And he visited them again on Boxing Day and on the 27th. Whether he sensed what was in the air, or whether he was just annoyed by the continued presence of Polly's male friend, a young chauffeur by the name of Leonard Miall, no one could tell. But the atmosphere in the house during those days was, to say the least, a little tense. And when Miall asked Polly if she would like to go for a ride, it exploded.

"You can't go," screamed de Vere, "you promised to go out with me."

"Come on, Eugene," said Miall, "it's only a little ride in the motor."

"She's not going," de Vere repeated.

"I'll do what I like," snapped Polly.

In the end, to avoid things getting worse, Miall decided to cancel the ride. Two days later, however, when Miall asked Polly to come to a dance, de Vere started up again. "She can't go on breaking her promise," he yelled. "If you do go I will follow you and make trouble. I hope you know how to fight."

Polly told Eugene not to make a fuss. But it didn't do any good. Even when she and Miall walked out of the door de Vere was still shouting: "You've played me up for the last time."

On New Year's Eve, Mrs Walker, Frank, Polly, Miall and de Vere went to the church of St. Martin's in the Fields to see the New Year in. As usual, the outing was preceded by a quarrel and, for the whole evening, bad temper seemed to reign. They returned home at 1 a.m. and displayed little of the joys of the season.

The next morning, Mrs Walker was up at six, preparing breakfast. She took Polly's to her bedroom and then, at about ten past eight, went to work. Before leaving she shouted up to her daughter not to go to sleep again because she, herself, had to be at work in half an hour.

At 1 p.m. Mrs Walker returned home, and was surprised not to receive her usual greeting from Polly. Going to Polly's bedroom, she found her daughter lying dead on the floor, her head battered and a silk stocking tied tightly round her neck.

Detectives called to the scene found that Polly had been struck on the head six times by a poker and a pair of tongs. The blows had been delivered with such force that the tongs had been broken in two.

Thrown over a chair at the foot of the bed was a man's overcoat containing keys which fitted the lodgings of de Vere. He, at once, became the prime suspect and was, in due course, arrested.

At his Old Bailey trial, de Vere admitted to killing Polly Walker but declared that it was not murder.

De Vere's counsel told the court that his client had asked him to say on his behalf: "I may have been weak, I may have been jealous. I was torn with anxiety and jealousy.. I have already lost everything dear to me in the world, and I would suffer the extreme penalty gladly but that I look with a spark of hope that a jury of my fellow-countrymen will not brand me as a murderer."

The jury to which Eugene de Vere had appealed were unmoved. They found him guilty of murder. Despite a petition for a reprieve submitted by leading public figures in de Vere's home country of Scotland, the one-legged beggar by day, dandy by night, was executed at Wandsworth Prison on March 25th, 1926.

26

SLEEPING STRANGLER

It wasn't a pretty sight. The lorry driver had just pulled off the road at Ridgewell, Essex to stretch his legs when he saw, in the sunlight, something gleaming under the bushes, in a ditch. He walked over to take a better look and his blood ran cold. What he was seeing was the sunlight shining on a dead girl's bright scarlet fingernails.

The girl must have been in her late teens or early twenties, a slender, full-bosomed brunette who, in life, must have been very attractive. In death, her body presented several unusual aspects.

The corpse lay straight and stiff, head-foremost down the slope of the ditch, the hands at the sides, the head partially in the water at the bottom of the ditch. The hair was short, like a man's. She wore a red satin party dress, but no coat. She was without shoes or stockings. The skirt of her dress had fallen away from her body enough to reveal that she was wearing no underwear.

The coroner's report did nothing to explain the mystery. It just made it deeper. He estimated that the girl had been dead 48 hours, or a little longer. But the body had been exposed to the elements for 12 hours or less. Her dress had not been put on normally, it appeared that she had been clothed by her killer. Her hair cut was also probably done by the murderer, clumsily and after she was dead.

That afternoon, a description of the dead girl was

repeated hourly on the radio. It was also sent to the national press. Initially, there was no response. But then, early in the evening, the police received a call from a Mrs Frances Constable.

Mrs Constable was pale and nervous as she admitted the officers into her home. "I heard over the radio about the dead girl," she said. "My daughter Jean has not been home since Saturday noon, when she left to go to a party. I'm terribly worried..."

She left the sentence unfinished as the officers showed her the red dress. She trembled uncontrollably as she stared at it. Then tears sprang to her eyes. For a moment, she turned away, weeping. Then she dried her eyes. "That dress belonged to my daughter, I'm certain of it," she said quietly. "But I can't understand what could have happened to Jean. Where did she go on Saturday? What was she doing over at Ridgewell?"

An investigation then began to try and trace the movements of Jean Constable during those fateful hours before her death.

Saturday had been New Year's Eve and Jean had intended to go to a party in Holland Park, London. In the end, however, she hadn't gone. Instead she had spent most of her time in the pubs closer to her home, in Braintree, Essex.

Jean had spent at least part of the evening at The Bell, a pub that had become extremely popular with the US servicemen from the nearby army base at Weathersfield. She had been seen there in the company of a Englishman, a good-looking fellow, tall and blonde and about 25-years-old.

This man was quickly traced and admitted that he had been with Jean on Saturday night. They had gone with a man called Mac and stayed with him. It was from his flat that Jean had disappeared.

Tracking down the mysterious Mac proved no easy task. Jean's friend had known he was from the American air base, but he couldn't remember the location of his flat nor did he know the man's real name. Eventually, however, his identity was revealed. "Mac" was a 27-year-old staff-sergeant with the American Air Force, a married man with two children. His name was Willis Boshears.

Boshears was clearly the prime suspect in the case and when the police visited him at the air base they read him his rights.

Boshears looked anxiously about the room and then smiled faintly: "I'm ready to make a statement, I'll tell you what I know."

A stenographer was summoned and Boshears dictated a long and detailed account of his activities over the weekend. He said how he had grown lonesome, with his wife away, so he had decided to spend New Year's Eve with friends at The Bell. There he had met Jean Constable, whom he had known since September, and also her English friend.

Boshears said that all three of them had gone back to his flat for a small party. They had hoped that others would join them, but no one did. As the hours passed by they were feeling tired and so he put a mattress in the floor. Jean Constable then undressed, rolled herself in a blanket and went to sleep on it. Boshears, according to his statement, said that after the man had gone he lay down beside her and he, too, dozed off.

"Next thing I remember is someone scratching my face," he said. "I opened my eyes. Jean was lying there under me and I had my hands around her throat. Then I realised she was dead."

"I'd been very drunk, but that sobered me a little. I carried Jean's body into the spare bedroom and locked the door. Then I went back to the mattress and lay down again, trying to think what to do. But I fell asleep."

Boshears said he spent most of Sunday and Monday trying to figure out how to get rid of the body. He decided to take it somewhere in his car. But he was afraid that the neighbours would see him carrying a woman out of his house. So he cut the girl's hair like a man's. He planned to dress her in an Air Force uniform. He reasoned that this would look as if he was taking back a drunken buddy.

Later, however, he abandoned the plan. Instead he clothed Jean's body in her dress. At about 11.30 on Monday night, he bundled her into a heavy coat, carried her to his car and drove out to Ridgewell. After leaving the body in the ditch, he returned home and burned the girl's coat, handbag, shoes, stockings and underwear. He kept her wristwatch and ten shillings from her handbag. These he now took from his pocket and handed to the officer.

At his trial on February 17th, 1961, Boshears stuck to his story about being asleep during the murder. And it proved to be an excellent defence. The eminent pathologist, Dr Francis Camps, was asked whether it was possible that the prisoner could have strangled Jean Constable in his sleep. He didn't say it was likely but neither was he able to say it was impossible. It was not beyond the bounds of belief.

Boshears defence made much of this during the trial and the judge also gave it emphasis. In summing up he directed the jury to consider that, if the defendant had strangled the girl while he was asleep, then it was not a voluntary action and would thus justify an acquittal. Furthermore, he told the jurors that if they were in any doubt at all as to whether or not Boshears was asleep, then he was also entitled to be acquitted.

The jury took precisely one hour and 50 minutes to come to a decision. Boshears was found not guilty.

The serviceman smiled broadly. He smiled again later that day when a US Air Force spokesman confirmed that he would face no further action from the military authorities.

In July, however, having returned to the United States, Willis Eugene Boshears was abruptly dismissed from the Air Force. His discharge was officially termed "dishonourable."

27

THE LEFT-HANDED KILLER

The girl was blonde, pretty and young, Her body was seductively curved, and she wore a shade too much make-up. Her name was Nina Ward and her morals were not those of a Sunday school teacher.

On a cold night in February 1942 Nina was working in a nightclub in the West End of London when a man who called himself Bill came up to her table.

"If you're as thirsty as you're beautiful," he said, "you must be dying for a drink. Let me buy you one."

The girl laughed. "Sit down," she said.

Within two hours, Nina and the man named Bill were talking and laughing like old friends. It was then that Bill suggested they buy a bottle and adjourn to the girl's flat. Nina thought that a brilliant suggestion. He was certainly handsome, with what looked like a good physique. How lucky, she thought, to have picked up Bill.

At 8.30 on the following Tuesday morning a meter reader for the electricity board stopped on his rounds at 153 Wardour Street. He climbed up a flight of stairs and knocked on the door. There was no response. But the door was slightly ajar so he thrust his head around the jamb: "Is anyone in?"

No one answered, but in the dim light he saw a figure lying prostrate on the wide divan bed in the middle of the room. He took his torch from his pocket and flicked it on.

A woman's body, dressed in a nightgown, was gruesomely spotlighted. She lay on her back with her head lolling over one edge of the bed, a leg hanging over the other. There was blood on the body, blood on the bed, blood on the floor.

He raced downstairs to the optician's shop on the ground floor. From there he dialled 999.

Within 20 minutes, Detective Inspector Horace Gray, Sergeant Ronald Others and a uniformed officer were on the scene.

A swift examination of the corpse revealed that the throat had been cut and the torso stabbed several times. Three incriminating weapons were on the bed itself. Near the girl's head lay a bloody razor blade and equally bloody curling tongs. At the bed's foot was a tin-opener. This, too, was badly bloodstained. A drawer of the dressing table had been forced open and a handbag lay on the floor. Its contents, which included a purse, were strewn nearby. The purse, however, contained no money.

This was the second gruesome murder in two days. Another corpse had been found in an air raid shelter the previous night. This too had been a woman, an Evelyn Hamilton. Miss Hamilton had been strangled and there were bruises on her chest indicating that her killer had knelt on her as he choked her. It was a different syle of murder, but equally gruesome.

At the time there was no reason to link the two killings. But soon that was to change. During the autopsy it was discovered that, whilst it had appeared that Nina Ward had been stabbed to death, in fact she had also been strangled. Furthermore, the pathologists deduced that both victims had been killed by someone who had been left-handed.

It was still too early to make a definite connection. But, on the third night, when a third body was found, the police began to be seriously concerned that a multiple killer was on the loose.

Margaret Lowe, an attractive 43-year-old widow and a prostitute, lived alone in a flat in Gosfield Street in the West

End. Her 14-year-old daughter had been evacuated to the provinces.

On Friday at 4 o'clock in the afternoon, Mrs Lowe's daughter had come to town to pay her fortnightly visit. As the girl approached the door of the Gosfield Street flat, she heard the whining of her mother's Scotch terrier. She rang the doorbell, but received no answer. Then she rang the bell of a neighbour. The woman told her that Mrs Lowe had not been seen for three days and that the dog had been howling for a long time. At the neighbour's suggestion the girl went downstairs and summoned a policeman.

The officer obtained a key from the landlord and unlocked the door of the flat. The dog barked joyfully when they entered.

Inside, lying absolutely naked on her bed, was Mrs Lowe. A silk stocking was tied tightly around her neck and everything was covered with blood. A razor blade, used to mutilate her body, lay on the floor, as did a bloodstained knife and a candle.

It was the third body in as many nights. Would there be a fourth?

The night manager of a hotel in Sloane Square lived with his wife, Doris, some distance from his work at Paddington. It was his custom to dine each night with his wife and set out for his job at 10 p.m. He had left as usual on Thursday night and then, on Friday morning, some three hours after the body of Margaret Lowe had been found, he returned to his home. He saw that his wife had not taken in the morning's milk. When he entered the flat, he also noticed that the previous night's dishes had not been cleared away.

He tried the bedroom door and found it locked from the inside. With the aid of a hammer he managed to smash the door open. As the lock gave way and he was able to look inside, his blood turned to ice.

Doris Jouannet lay on her back on the bed. She was dressed in a flimsy dressing gown which was open. Her own stocking was wrapped cruelly about her neck. She had been horribly slashed and mutilated. The instrument of her torture, a bloody razor blade, lay on the top of the dressing table.

Dazed, he picked up the telephone and put through a call to Scotland Yard.

The Jouannets had been married for six years and, according to Jouannet, the marriage had been a fine one. But a check on the dead woman revealed their marital life had not been quite what he thought it was.

Unknown to her husband, Doris Jouannet had led a wild life while he attended to his duties at the hotel. It had been her practice to frequent Leicester Square pubs mixing with the uniformed men who congregated there. She too had been a prostitute.

Now there were four corpses. It was as though a new Jack the Ripper was on the loose. Urgent action was called for.

A dozen of London's best looking policewomen were asked to wear revealing dresses, ordered to use triple their usual amount of make-up and were sent out into Piccadilly as decoys. The girls had no trouble at all in being picked up. However, none of them were approached by the man Scotland Yard were looking for. Instead, the first break in the case came purely by chance.

Early that evening a delivery boy was carrying a case of wine to the rear entrance of the Captain's Cabin pub near St. Alban's Street in the West End. Like everyone else during the strict wartime blackout, the boy carried a torch. He had just come out into the narrow street after making his delivery when he heard a fearful scream. He whipped his torch from his pocket and touched the button.

The halo of light revealed a young girl lying on the pavement with a man bending over her. The man blinked at the sudden light, then turned and sped away. The boy raced to the side of the girl and helped her to her feet.

"He tried to kill me," she sobbed, "Help me get to the police."

The boy did so and left the girl, Margaret Hayward, in their charge.

She said that she had met her attacker in a bar. He had

approached her and offered to buy a round of drinks. After these she had invited him to her flat and, on the way, they had stopped in a doorway.

"We began to make love and he kissed me," she said, "But then he put his hands around my throat and started to strangle me. I managed to scream. He held on to my throat with one hand and hit me with the other. I fell down. Then the boy turned on his torch and the man ran away."

"Which hand did he hit you with?" she was asked, "The left or the right?"

"The left, I think," said Miss Hayward, "He hit me on the right side of my face."

Margaret Hayward gave a full description of her assailant. He was wearing a RAF uniform, was about thirty years old and had blond hair and blue eyes.

The police then returned to the spot where she had been attacked. There they found Miss Hayward's purse on the ground, empty. But they found something else that was much more valuable. It was a Royal Air Force gas-mask. Clearly stencilled on the bag, which contained it, was the name Cummins and the service serial number 5259878.

Leading Aircraftman Gordon Frederick Cummins, the owner of the gas-mask, was picked up at the air cadets centre in St. John's Wood the following day. He denied any knowledge of the murders. The gas-mask, he said, was his but it had been lost, though he had forgotten to report it.

Routine investigation soon revealed that Cummins was an odd character. At 28 he was married and the father of one son. His wife insisted that their home was extremely happy and she never had any reason to suspect her husband of infidelity. His colleagues at the cadet base, however, told a different story.

"He's a phoney," said one of his hut mates. "He uses an imitation Oxford accent and told us he was entitled to use the word 'honourable' before his name because he is the illegitimate son of a member of the House of Lords. Around here we call him The Count."

On one occasion Cummins was said to have handed

around a photograph of the Queen being assisted into her car by a member of the Peerage. Cummins had said that this was his father. Actually Cummins, senior, was the superintendent of a school for delinquent boys.

Cummins constantly boasted of his romantic conquests. He talked, too, of the large amounts of money he spent and this claim had more substance. Said one of his colleagues: "I've seen him throw away ten pounds in a single night in bars and restaurants. That's more than two months' pay for us."

By now, the police were pretty sure where Cummins got all that money from. When Gordon Cummins' fingerprints were found to match those that had been left on the tin-opener and the mirror in Nina Ward's flat, they had no doubts.

Gordon Cummins was arrested and charged with the murders of Evelyn Hamilton, Doris Jouannet, Margaret Lowe and Nita Ward.

In due course he appeared in court where, after all the evidence was heard, the jury took less than an hour to return a verdict of guilty.

Gordon Cummins was hanged at Wandsworth early on the morning of June 25th, 1942, a time when all the erring girls of Piccadilly were still sound asleep.

28

CYANIDE FOR BREAKFAST

"I am impatient to have you back. I intend to do my best and perhaps to suffer in silence to keep the peace. I want you both back here, pronto."

As a love letter it left much to be desired. But it was enough to tempt 21-year-old Moira Burdett, to return with her child to her husband's flat in Appleford Road, North Kensington, London and give their marriage a second chance. If she had known what lay in store, however, she might have thought again. Just six months later, on November 27th, 1956, Moria Burdett was dead.

She collapsed at breakfast time, after drinking the tea that her husband had so kindly brewed. She was dead before the ambulance arrived. Indeed, as the post-mortem revealed, she had been dead for more than an hour before the ambulance was even summoned. Cyanide was the cause. A lethal dose was found in her stomach.

From the start, Brian Burdett was the prime suspect. It seemed so obvious he was the culprit that detectives half expected, a confession. But if that was what they expected they were sorely disappointed. Burdett insisted that he had not killed his wife.

Burdett admitted that some time before his wife died, he had stolen the poison from his work. But it was not to kill her, he maintained. It was to kill himself. "I felt they would be better without me," he said, "I felt responsible for my wife's listless and tired condition and thought that, if I killed myself, she would be free to marry again and start a new life."

He said that, after breakfast, he had seen his wife fall to the floor. He asked her what the matter was, but got no response. Going to fetch a cup of water for her, he saw the empty cyanide bottle and a cup at the side of the sink.

It was, he claimed, a great shock to him. Not wanting it to be known that his wife had committed suicide, he thought he might be able to conceal it. He threw what was left of the liquid in the cup away and put the bottle in his pocket.

Burdett also recalled that he threw away a pot of tea and a cup that was nearly full. He said he had cleaned the inside of the pot with a wire-wool pad and then washed all the cutlery and crockery.

The detectives were not impressed with Burdett's testimony and charged him with murder. In due course he appeared at the Old Bailey.

Though the prosecution insisted the the idea was utterly absurd, Brian Burdett's defence counsel pursued the claim of suicide tenaciously. At one point it even seemed that the jury would be swayed. Stressing the lack of motive for killing, Mr Ryder Richardson declared that although suicide might appear unlikely, the idea that Mrs Burdett had been murdered by her husband was more unlikely still. "The jury must be certain beyond doubt," he said, "that Burdett had deliberately and maliciously killed his wife and surely this cannot be done."

Sadly for Brian Burdett, however, it could. The jury had no doubts at all and delivered a verdict of guilty.

Brian Burdett was convicted of the murder of his wife and sentenced to death. That sentence was eventually commuted to life in prison.

29

THE OXFORD STREET
SHOOTING

Jacques Adrian Tratsart was an unfortunate young man. Unmarried and living alone in Norbury, south London, he was a depressive and a hopeless insomniac. Every night he would be wide awake, thinking dark thoughts and brooding on his fate. There were few people that Jacques liked, but there was no one he hated more than his father. It was his father on whom he blamed all the ills of the world.

A shoemaker by trade, John Tratsart was a Belgian who came to England just before the First World War. He had six children by his wife before she died in 1937. Then he married his housekeeper. This "act of betrayal," as his son Jacques saw it, was an unforgivable sin.

When the Second World War broke out the Tratsart family was evacuated to Northampton; all save 21- year-old Jacques, who was a toolmaker and therefore had a "reserved occupation." He was left in London to contribute to the war effort and brood over his father and the fact that the rest of the family had given tacit approval to the new marriage.

This arrangement continued until the end of the war, when the family in Northampton began contemplating a return to the capital. It was arranged that Jacques would meet his father, now aged 57, his brother Hugh, and two of his sisters, Claire, 28, and Anne, 13, at the Lyons Corner House in Oxford Street. Also present would be his aunt, the middle-aged sister of his father's first wife, a Miss Coemans. They were due to discuss the impending reunion.

The Lyons Corner House was one of many such eating places. These restaurants were a common feature of every major city in England and had flourished since the first one opened in Piccadilly in 1884. They enjoyed their greatest vogue between the two world wars, the chain of Lyons Corner House growing to no less than 250 establishments, which were only gradually phased out in the 1960s. As restuarant-cum-tearooms they gave the ordinary man in the street the opportunity to visit a restaurant and be waited on for a few pence. The waitresses, in their smart black and white uniforms, were known as "nippies," and the Lyons Corner House was the ideal meeting-place for friends, lovers and family members. One of the most famous of these Lyons Corner Houses was the one in London's Oxford Street, near Tottenham Court Road. A playwright might have used it as the setting for a romantic comedy; in fact this particular restaurant became the setting for murder.

The restaurant was crowded as the family of six sat around a table talking. They were all engaged in animated discussion, laughing and chatting, and few would have thought that the young man in spectacles who was fiddling around with something under the table had anything sinister in mind. Then the six shots rang out.

The babble of conversation in the crowded restaurant came to a sudden halt. In the hushed silence three members of the family were seen to fall, with blood pouring from wounds in their heads and bodies. The young man in spectacles stood over them, a smoking pistol in his hand.

As members of the public began to scream and hide themselves under the tables, two soldiers seized Jacques Tratsart and marched him towards the door. He made no attempt to struggle.

Jacques Tratsart was taken to Tottenham Court Road police station and questioned while he sipped a cup of tea. He spoke quite freely and without any sign of emotion or remorse. He admitted having planned to shoot his family and having purchased the pistol for that purpose. "The opportunity," he declared "only comes once, they say. It's best to be prepared."

Tratsart told the police that he had loaded the pistol with six bullets and had intended to kill his brother Hugh and his sister Claire as well as his father before also killing himself.

"I sat in the right position so that nobody could interfere with me shooting them and myself. We all sat talking normal gossip and then I got the gun out. I decided to shoot Claire first, then my father, then Hugh, then myself. I pointed the gun across the table at Claire and pulled the trigger. But nothing happened. I didn't know you had to pull the top back."

"Hugh saw me and grinned. Ten minutes later I repeated the performance and pulled harder at the trigger. But still nothing happened. This time the whole family saw me. I had the gun only about two feet from Claire. Yet they still had no idea that I was trying to kill them. When my aunt asked what I had in my hand, I said: 'Only a water-pistol,' and they seemed to believe me. They joked about it.

"But then I carried my plan through. I fired two bullets at Claire. I then fired two at my father and two at Hugh, coming round in a line. I was then standing up and pointed the gun at my head. But there were no bullets left."

Miraculously Jacques' brother Hugh survived the attack, though he sustained a horrific injury to his jaw. But his father died almost immediately and Claire died on the way to hospital. Jacques Tratsart was charged with double murder and attempted murder.

Doctors who examined him in prison declared that Jacques Tratsart was insane and thus unfit to plead. He was sent to Broadmoor where he learned how to play tennis and the piano. He also began to write a book about his father which he was still working on when he died of natural causes two years later.

His was obviously a case where mercy indicated that he should be regarded as someone not responsible for his actions - as much a victim as the people he slew. Jacques Tratsart was a mentally deranged young man who, finding the world an inequitable place, attempted to change it - with fatal consequences.

30

I'VE JUST CUT
ROSIE'S HEAD OFF

Elderly Mrs Amelia Tanton lived at 34 Cross Street, in the heart of Chatham's red light district. Her neighbour was Rose Smith, a 41-year-old mother of three whose husband was a naval officer, serving abroad.

In September 1926, Rose Smith began an affair with Harry Thompson, a 36-year-old miner who had come up from Wales to seek his fortune. He was a rough man who had already deserted his wife and five children, but he and Rose seemed to get on well enough and they enjoyed each other's company.

It wasn't long, however, before the quarrels began. Shouts and screams were frequently heard from their house and Mrs Tanton would often be disturbed by the sounds of slammed doors and smashed crockery.

On the evening of February 8th, another row erupted, even noisier than usual.

"At about 9.30," Mrs Tanton was later to say, "one of three children - a girl of about eight - ran screaming from the house and said to me, 'Uncle Harry's got hold of my mum's neck and is choking her'."

Mrs Tanton didn't pay much attention to this, but when the other children, obviously frightened out of their wits, came running from the house she took them into her home and put them to bed.

A few minutes later a nightmarish scream echoed from

next door. It was heard by Mrs Tanton. It was heard also by Frederick George Garrett, who lived at number 38. He immediately rushed to his neighbour's house to find out what had happened.

As he walked into the front room, it was clear that a fight had taken place. Furniture lay all about and broken china ornaments were strewn across the floor. Only when he reached the kitchen, however, did Garrett witness the true horror of the battle.

"By the light of an oil lamp on the table I saw Mrs Smith lying on the floor, all crumpled up and covered in blood. There was a nasty, bloody mess on her neck and a pool of blood by her head." Police investigators would later reveal that Rose Smith's head had been almost completely severed from her body.

As Garrett made this gruesome discovery, the murderer was walking cheerily down Chatham's High Street. It was like a scene from Monty Python.

Harry Thompson was barefoot and appeared to the worse for drink. Spying a friend of his across the road, he went over to greet him.

"Hello, George," he said, " I've just cut Rosie's head off."

"I didn't know whether to believe him or not," George Varney subsequently told the jury at Kent Assizes. "But I told him I would go with him until we met a copper. We soon found one at the bottom of Clover Street, and I said to the policeman, "Here is a man who says he's cut a woman's head off."

During his trial Thompson sat rocking gently to and fro on his chair. He claimed to have no recollection of anything that happened between 4 p.m. on February 8th and his arrival at the police station, but he accepted that the witnesses were telling the truth.

On being found guilty and sentenced to death, Harry Thompson said: "Thank you," turned quickly and almost ran down the flight of steps leading to the cells. He was hanged on March 9th, 1926, precisely one month after he had taken Rose Smith's life.

31

THE STRANGE STORY OF POST BOY

Although not included on many maps of Ohio, the small town of Post Boy has an intriguing history, for it is believed to be the only town in the world named after a murder.

It began on an autumn afternoon in 1825 in Booths Tavern, located on the road between Cadiz and Coshocton. A stranger entered the bar and ordered drinks all round. There could be no quicker way to win friends, and William Johnson, with his city manners and smart clothes, was soon being acclaimed by the locals as one of their own.

The atmosphere in the tavern became even more convivial with the arrival of young William Cartmell. As the rural mail carrier, Cartmell was a very welcome visitor and his arrival was always a happy occasion for the news-starved residents of the frontier area.

But Cartmell didn't stay long. After handing out the mail and downing a few goblets of rum, he said he would have to be going. William Johnson offered to ride with him as far as Coshocton. The post boy, grateful to have some company, accepted eagerly.

The crowd had barely bade the men goodbye and resumed their drinking when Johnson returned. His face was pale, his eyes dilated with fear. "Come quick," he said breathlessly, "Somebody's shot the post boy. I think he's dead."

While one of the men rode to New Philadelphia to fetch

Sheriff Walter Blake, the others followed Johnson to a wooded spot about two miles away. There Cartmell lay sprawled on his face, a bullet in his back. A glance was enough to tell them that he was dead. His horse was grazing nearby, but the saddlebags containing his mail were gone.

"What happened?" someone asked Johnson.

Johnson explained that he was riding with the post boy when he decided to have a drink from a small stream. Cartmell, meanwhile, said he would ride slowly so that Johnson could catch him up.

"I was stooped over, drinking, when I heard a shot," he went on, "I jumped on my horse and hurried down the track. I found him like he is now. While I was bending over him, a man came out of the woods and asked what had happened. When I told him, he suggested that I come and tell you fellows at the tavern, while he went over the hill there and roused a neighbour."

"There ain't nobody living over there," said one of the men suspiciously.

"What did he look like?" asked another.

"He was a dark man, about 25 years old," said Johnson. "He was stockily built and carried a rifle."

By the time Sheriff Blake arrived from New Philadelphia the men's opinion of Johnson was openly hostile. When the sheriff examined Johnson's rifle and found that it had been recently fired cries of "lynch him" were heard. But Blake quickly stilled the disturbance and led the newcomer to the jail.

Later that day John Smeltzer, a drover from Oxford township, rode into town. Seeing all the commotion he went over to the sheriff's office.

"What are you doing around here, John?" enquired Blake.

Smeltzer explained that he was returning from Pittsburgh where he had delivered several hundred head of cattle. His saddlebags, he said, contained more than $1,000 in silver.

While he was talking, Blake noticed that Smeltzer's

horse and saddlebags looked exactly like Cartmell's. The two men even resembled each other.

At that moment Blake realised what had happened. The hold-up man had mistaken the post boy for Smeltzer! Cartmell carried nothing valuable in his bags, only ordinary mail. The drover, on the other hand, had $1,000 in silver, which in those days was a fortune.

Johnson, then, was innocent, for he knew that Cartmell wasn't the drover. The killer had to be someone else. But who could that someone be?

Questioned closely, Smeltzer could think of no one who wished him harm. But he had to admit that many people knew when and by what route he would be travelling, and many of them knew he was carrying silver. If he were to try and single out a suspect, he said, he'd have to put the finger on every male resident in Tuscarawus County.

Blake was now absolutely certain that Johnson was innocent, but there was nothing he could do. Despite the testimony he made on the stranger's behalf, William Johnson was taken to New Philadelphia and charged with the post boy's murder.

Johnson went on trial a month later. He was found guilty and sentenced to hang.

Blake was at his wits' end as the day of the hanging drew near and he questioned Johnson again and again. But it was all to no avail.

"This man you spoke to after the shooting, would you know him if you saw him again?" he asked.

Johnson nodded. "I'm sure of it, sheriff," he said. "I'd never forget that face."

Shaking his head, Blake went to see James Patrick, a former judge and one of the shrewdest lawyers on the frontier.

"Isn't there something we can do, Jim?" he inquired helplessly. "That man is as innocent as you are."

Patrick thought for several moments. "Does Johnson still insist he saw a dark complexioned man right after the shooting?" he asked.

Blake nodded. "Yes, but that doesn't prove anything, The real killer will give New Philadelphia a wide berth, at least until after the hanging, anyway."

Patrick removed a dusty law book from the shelf and pointed to a passage. "It says here," he said gravely, "that, as sheriff, you have the power to order everyone in the county to appear at the hanging. Failure to comply means a jail sentence."

Blake understood what the learned judge meant and wasted no time to make it work. Within an hour he had couriers riding into every remote section of the county with orders that every male person must appear on Broadway Street, the scene of the hanging, two days hence.

On the fatal morning more than three hundred persons lined both sides of the narrow, dusty street and, at exactly 10 o'clock, Sheriff Blake emerged with his pale but now hopeful prisoner.

As Johnson walked slowly towards the gallows in the centre of the street, he scrutinised each face at length.

Halfway down the line he suddenly stiffened. Blake followed his gaze and saw a young man of around 25, garbed in buckskin. The man flushed and lowered his eyes.

"That's the man!" cried Johnson, "He's the one who shot the post boy."

The man turned to flee but was quickly overpowered. Hustled into Blake's office, he said he was John Funston, a squatter. Sullenly admitting his guilt, he claimed he had mistaken the post boy for John Smeltzer. The mail bags were found near his home a few hours later.

John Funston went on trial on November 16th, 1825, and was found guilty. He was sentenced to death by Judge Harmer on November 19th and hanged on December 30th.

In memory of the death of William Cartmell, the town has been called Post Boy ever since.

32

A CRUEL SILENCE

Mona Lilian Tinsley had not returned home from school that afternoon of January 5th, 1937, and her mother was worried. It was 4.30 and the streets were already growing dark. With the front door open behind her Mrs Tinsley peered each way along the narrow road. Her ten-year-old daughter was nowhere to be seen.

Past 4.30! Mona should be back by now. From the doorway of her home at No. 11 Mrs Tinsley continued to gaze worriedly into the dim distances of Thoresby Road, Newark, South Yorkshire. The girl was hardly ever later than half-past four, and the Methodist School in Guildhall Street, was barely 20 minutes' walk away, even for Mona's lingering feet.

The Tinsleys' other children had already sat down for their tea. Sensing their mother's anxiety they were not their usual selves. They ate in utter silence.

The meal came to an end at last, but still without Mona. Mrs Tinsley sent one of the older children out to look for her. The child returned, only to report searching everywhere and seeing her nowhere.

Time dragged by, until there came a clatter at the door. But it wasn't Mona, it was Wilfred, her father.

"Mona's not home from school!" his wife exclaimed.

Tinsley's seamed and rugged face tautened as he heard the news.

Without staying for a bite or drink, Wilfred Tinsley went out again. The school was closed and dark, but he found the caretaker and spoke to him. He had heard nothing. Tinsley also called at several sweet-shops and everywhere else where he thought Mona might be. All without success. Extremely anxious now, he went to the police station.

An officer went back with him to Thoresby Road, but Mona was still not there when they arrived. Tinsley sank dejectedly into a chair.

The policeman noted the date, and took a description of the child, together with a photograph. He left with reassuring remarks and a search for Mona was launched.

That morning the presence of a policeman in their classroom quietened the wide-eyed children at the Methodist School. He was asking questions about Mona. An 11-year-old boy, Willie Plackett, said that he had seen Mona near the bus stop after school the previous day.

Gently the officer extracted from him what little the boy might know. Mona had been waiting at the Guildhall Street bus stop, it appeared, the one in the same street as the school, where the buses leave for Retford. Was she alone? No, she seemed to be with a man. Was she talking to him? Yes, she was. What did the man look like? The boy described him as best he could. He had strange, staring eyes, he said. Would he know this man again? Yes, he would know him. The time? Willie Plackett said it was about 4.30 - maybe later.

Armed with this vague description, police officers promptly began questioning bus conductors. Quite soon they struck lucky. Charles Reville, the conductor on the 4.45 bus from Newark remembered that a man with a small, ginger, Hitler-style moustache, a long face and slightly hooked nose had taken a little girl with him on the bus. They had alighted at Retford. The little girl was wearing a brown tweed coat and a blue woollen suit, just like Mona.

The description of the man also matched one given by Mrs Annie Hird, who had seen him at the bus stop the previous day. She could also put a name to the face. He was Mr Fred Hudson, a car mechanic and lorry driver who, a short time before, had lodged at the Tinsley's house for a few weeks.

Fred Hudson, whose real name was Fred Nodder, was soon tracked down to a house called "Peacehaven" in Smeath Road, Hayton. There was clear evidence that a child had recently stayed at his home. Moreover, many more witness had now came forward to testify that they had seen Nodder and Mona Tinsley together.

At first Nodder insisted he had not seen the girl since he had left the Tinsley's home, but, as the evidence piled up, he began to change his story. Eventually he admitted taking Mona on the bus and bringing her to his home. Nodder claimed that Mona had asked to visit her aunt in Sheffield and he had agreed to help her. "I repented my action as soon as I started off" he said. He then related an implausible tale of letting her sleep the night in his bed whilst he slept on the couch and then, when morning had come, putting her on a bus to Sheffield. He said he had given her food, money and written directions to ensure she had a safe journey. He was sure that, by now, she was already with her aunt. Nobody believed him.

The police redoubled their efforts to find the little girl. The canal was dragged, so too was a river near Nodder's home. Nodders' house and garden were carefully examined. Widespread checks were made on hundreds of cars and lorries which had been in Retford on the night of January 6th. All the packages that had been checked in at railway baggage rooms within a 100-mile radius were examined. Trains were scanned, as were buses. But all to no avail.

On March 10th, 1937 Frederick Nodder appeared at Birmingham Assizes to answer for his actions. Feeling the case against him was not strong enough to guarantee a conviction for murder, the prosecution arraigned him on nine charges related to Mona's abduction. This, it was felt, would ensure Nodder's conviction and imprisonment pending the possible discovery of her body.

Tall, broad-shouldered and robust, Nodder took it all in his stride. He pleaded not guilty to everything. Those thin lips beneath his jutting clipped moustache, pressed together in a smile that seemed to challenge the law. He seemed utterly confident that he would be vindicated.

Witness after witness told how they had seen Mona Tinsley and Nodder together. The evidence against him was colossal. But Nodder remained impassive. His defence counsel brought no witness on his behalf, nor any evidence that could support him. They simply claimed that there was no case to answer.

The judge evidently disagreed.

"There is one person who knew what Mona Tinsley did, how she was provided for, and where she slept - if she slept at all - on the night of January 5th," Mr Justice Swift said in his summing up, "And he is silent. He says nothing at all. The witness box is open and free. Why did he not tell you?"

The jury had an answer. After less than 20 minutes' discussion they found Nodder guilty of abducting Mona Tinsley and he was sentenced to seven years' imprisonment.

But Mona was still missing, and her family and friends continued the hunt for her. Wilfred Tinsley was becoming ill with the strain and anxiety, but still he carried on. "I can't rest until I have found my child," he declared.

Mrs Estelle Roberts, a prominent London clairvoyant, was among many people who offered her services. From its beginning the case had interested her. Mona Tinsley, she said, had appeared to her soon after she was reported missing.

Mrs Roberts announced that Mona had told her how she had been strangled and placed in a sack, conveyed in something on wheels to the water and thrown in. As narrated by the medium, the child's account gave details of various landmarks along the route taken by her murderer.

Mrs Roberts said that Mona would not let her rest. The child was commanding her to find her corpse and avenge her death. The clairvoyant thus journeyed north to the scene of the crime and submitted herself to Mona Tinsley's ethereal will.

The Nodder house was now stripped of furniture, but on entering in the company of a police officer, Mrs Roberts described the former appearance of the interior with perfect accuracy. She then led the officer over the local landscape. It was strange to her, but one by one the landmarks of which she had spoken duly showed. Eventually they reached the River Idle.

That, without doubt, was Mona's grave, Mrs Roberts repeated.

Another medium was approached by the missing child's father himself. At Hykeham, near Lincoln, he sought out 72-year-old Mrs Lewin, whose reputation for solving crime mysteries was well established. She knew Wilfred Tinsley's name and business before he had even begun speaking to her.

In a trance she re-enacted the death of his daughter. The child would be found in the River Idle, she said. Wilfred Tinsley left the medium with her last words echoing in his head: "I have tasted the mud in my mouth."

In June, five months after Mona's disappearance, Walter Marshall, the manager of a local gasworks, took his family on a Sunday outing, sailing on the Idle. They were picnicking on the bank when Marshall saw, dimly wavering at the bottom of a shallow creek, the unmistakable remains of a child. Word was sent to Bawtry, half a mile away, and soon three police officers arrived in a boat. Together they raised the corpse to the surface.

As Mrs Lewin had suggested, the body had been held down by the head in the mud,

Wilfred Tinsley identified the body as that of his missing daughter, his wife breaking down at the inquest as Mona's faded, water-worn clothes were brought out for display.

A post-mortem examination revealed that the little girl had not drowned but, just as the clairvoyant had said, she had been strangled. She had been thrown into the river after death.

On November 22nd, Frederick Nodder stood once again in the dock. This time the charge was murder.

Unlike before, Nodder now chose to give evidence in his defence. But he found it impossible to answer any of the prosecution's questions. When they asked something of him he just stared back at his inquisitor for a long-drawn half-minute, without saying a single word. The court stared at him in a fascinated silence until, finally, Nodder lowered his gaze and closed his eyes.

Found guilty by the jury, Frederick Nodder was sentenced to death.

"Frederick Nodder, the jury by their verdict have found that you murdered Mona Lilian Tinsley," intoned the Judge. "Justice has slowly overtaken you, and it only remains for me to pronounce the sentence which the law and justice requires."

On December 30th, 1937, almost a year after Mona's death, Frederick Nodder was hanged at Lincoln Jail. No one mourned his death.

33

PALMER THE POISONER

William Palmer was born in Rugeley, Staffordshire, in August, 1824. His interest in practical medicine began in his youth, when he was hired by a firm of manufacturing chemists in Liverpool. Later he found work in a doctor's office and progressed from there to St. Bartholomew's Hospital, London, where he enrolled as a pupil in 1842.

In due course, Palmer qualified as a doctor and returned to Rugeley where he married one Ann Thornton, an attractive and rather wealthy lady from the neighbourhood.

In those early years Palmer built up a small practice and he and his wife seemed a contended couple. But, behind the scenes, all was not well. Palmer was a philanderer and his constant affairs put an enormous strain on their marriage. His wife's discovery of Palmer's illegitimate daughter, the result of an affair with a servant girl, did nothing to improve matters.

William Palmer had never shown much interest in the child, but suddenly he became overcome by paternal concern. He asked the girl's mother to bring her child to his surgery so that he might satisfy himself that his daughter was in good health. Until then, the young girl had been perfectly fit. One week after Palmer's "examination", however, she died.

This was but the first calamity that would befall Palmer's family and friends. Many more would follow.

By the end of 1849, Palmer, who had now graduated from being a philanderer to being also an inveterate gambler, was heavily in debt. Around this time he invited his wealthy mother-in-law to stay. She cheerfully agreed, but it would have been better if she had not. Within two weeks of her acceptance and arrival, she was dead.

Her heartbroken daughter benefitted considerably from the unexpected tragedy and so, consequently did her husband. However, it was evidently not enough because, a month or two later, another invitation was dispatched.

This one was sent to a bookmaker friend of his named Bladon, to whom the doctor owed £400. The bookmaker was invited to Rugeley for a short stay. He arrived in fine health and in possession of at least £100 in cash, as well as his private "betting book", which contained a detailed list of his debtors. A week later, a distraught Mrs Bladon arrived at the Palmer residence to find herself a widow. Her husband, the doctor informed her, had expired following days of severe stomach pains.

When she collected her dead husband's belongings, Mrs Bladon was surprised to discover that all that remained of his cash was £11 in notes and a few coins. Furthermore the "betting book," which she knew her husband always carried with him, was missing. Mrs Bladon's brother suggested that she should contact the police, not only about her husband's sudden and mysterious death but also about the missing property. Without more positive proof, however, the grieving Mrs Bladon refused to take the matter any further. Dr Palmer was left in peace.

Over the next three years, William Palmer continued to exude a curious aura of death. Two of his uncles died with identical symptoms after being "treated" by their nephew. Two of his own children were also struck down with a mysterious illness. An acquaintance named Bly, to whom Palmer had lost £800, was another to die in the doctor's care, his winnings vanishing as quickly as his good health.

By January 1854 Palmer had become far more ambitious than he was in his early days, and tried, for the first time, to increase the rewards of his medical work with a little help from the insurance business. He began with his wife.

Palmer arranged to take out a £3,000 insurance policy on his wife's life. Two months later, with a different insurer, he took out another in the sum of £5,000. In June of that year, with the help of a third insurance company, the total value of insurance was brought up to £13,000. From then on, it was inevitable that Ann Palmer's time on this earth would not last much longer.

She first complained of feeling unwell on September 20th, 1854 and took to her bed thinking it was no more than a common cold. Her husband, however, didn't take it so lightly. Next morning, displaying uncommon concern, he prepared her tea without milk and some dry toast and carried them to her room. His care was not wasted. Ann Palmer soon realised she was a good deal more poorly than she had first thought. She took only a little of the food and drink her husband had brought her and, within half an hour, was violently sick. Subsequent meals and drinks affected her no better.

After three days, when her condition still showed no improvement, Palmer thought it best to ask for a second opinion. He called in his colleague and family friend Dr Bamford, an 82-year-old, semi-retired physician. Bamford was bordering on senility, but he examined Mrs Palmer with diligent care. After prodding and probing her for a few minutes, his diagnosis was clear. "I think," declared the wise old man, "it may be cholera."

Palmer readily agreed with this verdict and asked Bamford to call again. The elderly doctor came back the following Tuesday, and the Friday too. By then, however, it was too late. Mrs Palmer was dead.

Wasting no time, Palmer had Bamford sign the death certificate, stipulating cholera as the cause of death. A further endorsement was supplied by Dr Knight, another friend of the family, who was also in his eighties. Knight took a little more persuading than his collegue, but only

because he was almost completely deaf and found it difficult to hear what Palmer was telling him. In due course,
however, he completed the certificate as he was supposed
to.

The insurance companies received notification of Mrs
Palmer's death with some suspicion. Indeed, there was
discussion about withholding full payment pending an
investigation. However, since the independent signatories
of the death certificate had registered no official misgivings
about the woman's death, the companies had little alterna-
tive but to pay out.

With money in his bank and his creditors paid off, Dr
Palmer was, for the first time in many months, entirely free
of debt. Alas, however, being a gambler, he was soon back
in his old predicament. But, as insurance had saved him the
last time he reasoned it may as well save him again. This
time he chose his good-natured brother, Walter, as the
victim.

Walter was as bad a gambler as his brother. He was also
an alcoholic. In Palmer's mind, therefore, he was the
perfect candidate. Palmer began to arrange for his brother's
life to be covered with six different insurance companies for
a total sum of £82,000. It would be a vast fortune for the
doctor to inherit and see him clear of all the difficulties that
he might face. Unfortunately, however, Dr Palmer had
underestimated the common sense of the insurance industry. When the prospective insurers discovered that the
policies were to cover an unemployed alcoholic, five of
them backed out immediately. Surprisingly though the
sixth, the Prince of Wales Insurance Company, were not
put off. Their policy valued at £12,000 was agreed.

With the Prince of Wales coverage secured, Palmer
wasted no time in carrying out the second stage of his plan.
He moved his brother to a house on the other side of
Stafford, away from inquisitive neighbours and, more
importantly, away from a certain Dr Waddell who had,
several times, tried to help the poor man, and set to work.

With uncharacteristic generosity, Palmer paid the rent

on his brother's new home and provided him with a small allowance for food. He also supplied a servant, Thomas Walkenden, to cater for Walter's alcoholic needs. Every evening Thomas would provide a bottle of gin for Walter to drink, and every morning too, the same would appear.

It didn't take long for Walter's health to deteriorate. Soon, almost skeletal and constantly racked by bouts of severe coughing, Walter was virtually bedridden and utterly dependent on his paid "bottle-holder." And yet, although his conditioned worsened by the week, his rate of deterioration hardly pleased his impatient brother. By August 12th, Palmer had had enough. He obtained an ounce of prussic acid from a wholesale chemist and, two days later, with a bottle of brandy in his hand and the poison in his pocket, he visited Walter Palmer for the very last time.

Palmer promptly registered his claim with the Prince of Wales Insurance Company and waited expectantly for their cheque. Alas, however, it never came. Palmer had been careful about his brother but not quite careful enough. The bothersome Dr Waddell had managed to keep in touch with his old patient and had expressed deep concern over his well-being. When he heard that Walter had died Waddell communicated his worries to the man's insurers. As a consequence, they told Palmer that not only would they be withholding payment on the policy, they had already instigated a thorough investigation of the case.

Palmer was furious. He was also desperate. His creditors were now moving in on him, and he had to find some money to fend them off.

At length he decided to try, once more, an insurance claim. This time his victim was a relative stranger, a farm worker named George Bate.

He approached Bate and put forward the proposal as a form of investment. George Bate was a simple minded fellow and cheerfully agreed. Palmer moved swiftly into action.

Describing his victim as "a gentleman and property owner" a policy, with the death value of £10,000, was provisionally accepted by the Midland Insurance Company. It was, however, soon rejected. Sadly for Palmer, though mercifully for Bate, once the insurance agent saw the labourer hoeing turnips on the farm, his life cover was abruptly cancelled.

Palmer would have to look elsewhere.

Thoroughly disillusioned with the insurance business, William Palmer now put his mind to obtaining money through other means. The new opportunity presented itself soon enough.

On November 13th, 1855, Dr Palmer attended the Shrewsbury Races in the company of John Parsons Cook. Palmer gambled heavily, but, not blessed with luck, he lost on every race. Not so his colleague, however. Cook not only won his bets but he had a horse of his own running in the 2 o'clock and the beast came in first. With between £700 and £800 in gambling winnings, and the handsome prize money for the race it had been a good day for John Cook. From then on Palmer hardly left his side.

To celebrate his winnings, Cook arranged a supper party at a nearby hotel. There was much fun and gaiety at the affair and Palmer was one of the happiest men there. Later in the evening he was seen taking a small bottle from his pocket and tipping its contents into Cook's brandy.

Before long, Cook was vomiting and, at Palmer's insistence, retired to one of the hotel bedrooms. Under the care of Dr Palmer John Cook lingered for nearly a week. But, in the early hours of Wednesday morning he finally passed away. Palmer expressed little in the way of grief. When one of the hotel cleaners entered Cook's room she too found Dr Palmer going through the corpse's pockets.

Cook's stepfather, William Vernon Stevens, arrived for the funeral on November 23rd. He was surprised to find that his step-son's diary, in which he kept all his financial transactions, was nowhere to be found. He was more surprised still when Dr Palmer approached him and proffered a document, purporting to be signed by John Cook, acknowledging a loan of £4,000 from William Palmer.

Stevens immediately suspected foul play and demanded a post-mortem.

Dr Palmer, though initially shocked, managed to regain his composure and, indeed, offered his services to the doctors who were to perform the examination. Alas, however, in the dissecting room, William Palmer was less than helpful. After Cook's stomach and intestines had been removed and put in a stone jar he "accidentally" stumbled against it. After it was retrieved he then hid it in a "safe place", just behind the door. Later a young messenger, employed to transport the stomach to London for examination, was paid £10 to drop it.

Despite all Dr Palmer's efforts, however, the examination was finally performed, and antimony, as well as the possibility of strychnine, was found in the horse owner's body.

As the inquest drew to a close all the evidence indicated "wilful murder." William Palmer emerged as the prime, indeed the only suspect.

When the news leaked out, quickly followed by stories of all the doctor's other crimes, a huge wave of hostility erupted against him. It was not safe for him to be in jail let alone stand in the dock of a Staffordshire court. The chances of William Palmer receiving a fair trial in the county were next to negligible.

As a consequence the "Palmer Act" was passed in Parliament, allowing him to have the trial moved elsewhere: to London.

Palmer was tried at the Old Bailey on May 14th, 1856. Since there was virtually no chance of his escaping his date with the executioner, the charges involved his wife and brother were not pursued. But he put up a brave fight. For eight hours his counsel pleaded his case. But it was all to no avail. In the end Palmer was found guilty of murder and sentenced to death.

Doctor William Palmer was hanged outside Stafford Gaol on June 14th, 1856. As he mounted the scaffold and the noose was tightened around his neck, the crowd that had gathered to witness his death all hissed in unison: "Poisoner!"

34

THE BOASTS OF
THOMAS CREAM

The remarkable career of Dr Cream predates his arrival in England by a good many years. Already in America and Canada he was a known murderer, a blackmailer and an abortionist. He had been convicted of one killing and seemed likely to be convicted of more. Even then he was known to be eccentric, callous and crazy. And yet it was not until he turned up on the streets of London in the autumn of 1891, that Cream's gruesome life-story became truly macabre.

By now he was 41 and, in all likelihood, suffering from tertiary syphillis. As a doctor he would have recognised the symptoms and, in his strange twisted mind, it may have been this that provided him with the justification to carry out his grisly campaign. For campaign it was: its aim to destroy the class of women who had sown the seeds of his own destruction.

Cream arrived in London on October 5th, 1891 and wasted no time in familiarising himself with its sordid gutter-life. He found lodgings at 103 Lambeth Palace Road and, dressed in top hat and long flowing cloak, cheerfully paraded through the squalid streets, where people lived on the brink of abject poverty.

Within a week Cream had already selected his first victims and headed off to Parliament Street where, at Priest's chemists, he bought some nux vomica, a preparation that contains a considerable quantity of strychnine. He signed the register "Thomas Neill, M.D." and gave his correct address. He also ordered some gelatine capsules, used for giving medicines. Priest's had none in stock, but promise to get them for him.

On the morning of October 13th, Ellen Donworth, a prostitute who lived at 8 Duke Street (now Duchy Street), received a letter from a client she only knew as "Fred." It invited her to meet him at 7 p.m. at the York Hotel, Waterloo Bridge Road. "Do not destroy this paper and envelope," it insisted, "Bring them with you." Cream was taking no chances on leaving written evidence.

Just 45 minutes after Ellen Donworth met Cream, his poison was already doing its work. A man standing outside the Wellington pub near Waterloo Station saw her as she staggered along the street. He watched as she collapsed against a wall, sliding down to fall on her face. He went to her aid and lifted her to her feet. In that unhappy neighbourhood, drunkenness was common enough, and he merely thought her staggering footsteps, her trembling and facial twitching was due to alcohol. He helped her to walk back to her home.

Soon, however, it was obvious that there was something much more seriously wrong with Miss Donworth. She began to have convulsions. Wide-eyed, frightened fellow-boarders watched her agonized squirming on her bed. And it took several people to hold her down.

In her lucid moments. before she was taken to hospital, Ellen gasped out: "A tall gentleman with cross eyes, silk hat and bushy whiskers gave me a drink twice out of a bottle with white stuff in it." But she could say little more. After hours of dreadful suffering and more convulsions, Ellen Donworth died. A post-mortem examination showed conclusively that strychnine had killed her.

The inquest was held at St. Thomas's Hospital - where Cream had once worked and studied - on October 15th. Just before the proceedings opened, the coroner, Mr G.P. Wyatt, received an astonishing letter:

"I am writing to say that if you fail to bring the murderer of Ellen Donworth to justice, I am willing to give you such assistance as will bring the murderer to justice, provided your Government is willing to pay me £300,000 for my services. No pay if not successful.

A. O'Brien, Detective"

Mr O'Brien's offer, however, was not accepted. The inquest returned a verdict that Ellen Donworth died "by poisoning with strychnine... by a person unknown."

A. O'Brien, of course, was Cream himself and, three weeks later, he sent another peculiar letter on the same subject. Addressed to Frederick Smith, M.P. son of W.H.Smith, the newsagent magnate, it came from a "Mr H. Baynes, barrister" and stated that "Mr Baynes" had incontrovertible proof that the politician had poisoned Ellen Donworth. The letter-writer said that he alone could save him, at a price, and instructed Mr Smith to put a notice in the window of W.H.Smith & Son's office in the Strand.

Rather than agree to these instructions, Frederick Smith, took the letter immediately to the police. They requested that he should, indeed, put a notice in the window and a careful watch was kept to see who might respond. But the mysterious "Mr Bayne" failed to appear and soon the operation was called off. After all, the police had other things to do. Already there had been another poisoning of a south London prostitute.

On October 19th, Matilda Clover a 27-year-old prostitute who, though a heavy drinker, still had a rugged beauty, received a letter from "Fred."

"Miss Clover, meet me outside the Canterbury. Please bring this paper and envelope with you. Yours, Fred"

Matilda went out - clean and sober - to keep the appointment. She had a few drinks with Cream, who then suggested: "Well, shall we go now?"

The girl nodded.

When they arrived back at Lambeth Road, the door was opened by Lucy Rose, a servant in the house. She saw Clover go out a little later for some bottled beer, while Cream waited in her room.

After Clover had returned and they were drinking the beer "Fred" brought the conversation round to the subject of pregnancy. Then, with a confidential smile, he took two capsules wrapped in tissue paper from his waistcoat pocket.

"These will fix you up," he told her, "Take these when you go to bed tonight. Then you won't have anything to worry about."

Matilda Clover would very soon have no further worries about anything. That night, just before blowing out her candle, she gulped down the capsules.

At 3 o'clock on the morning of October 20th, the house on Lambeth Road erupted into frenzy of activity. Matilda was screaming in unbearable agony. Lucy Rose and Mrs Vowels, the landlady, rushed up to Matilda's bedroom to find her lying, undressed, on her back across the bed. Her convulsions had been so violent that she had jammed her head between the bed and the wall. Between screams she sobbed out: "I'm so glad you've come! I've been calling a long time!"

Matilda had spells when the knifing pains eased. Then she was able to tell Mrs Vowles and Lucy Rose that it was the man called Fred who had poisoned her with his pills. But the attacks soon returned, and with increased violence. Mrs Vowels sent a messenger to get a local physician. Alas, the doctor refused to come. In his place, arrived Mr Choppin, his unqualified assistant. Choppin diagnosed Matilda's seizures as being an attack of delirum tremens.

Matilda Clover's death occured a little more than an hour later. There was no inquest, and soon afterwards, Miss Clover was buried in a pauper's grave at Tooting Cemetery.

At that point, no one other than Cream knew, or even

suspected, that Matilda had been poisoned. But that would soon be changed.

On October 22nd Thomas Cream, with that madness that was so peculiarly his, asked Emily Sleaper, his landlady's daughter to go down the road to number 27. "I knew a young woman there," he said, "I think she's been poisoned and I want to know whether she's dead." Emily refused to make the inquiry, whereupon Dr Cream muttered: "Perhaps it's just as well."

A month later, however, Cream could keep silent no longer. On November 30th, 1891, Dr William Broadbent, one of the most distinguished surgeons of the day, received a letter.

"Sir, Miss Clover who, until a short time ago, lived at 27 Lambeth Palace Road, S.E., died at the above address on October 20 (last month) through being poisoned with strychnine..."

It went on to demand £2,500 for suppression of the "evidence" against Dr Broadbent. And William Broadbent wasn't the only one to be accused. Countess Russell also received a similar missive at her suite in the Savoy Hotel. This time it was her husband, Lord Russell, who was claimed to be the poisoner.

Having stirred up this hornet's nest Cream now decided to take a short break from his activities. He travelled to Berkhamstead, where he met and married Laura Sabbatini, a highly respectable young woman. He also voyaged back to Canada to convert into ready cash some of the stocks and shares that had been left to him by his father. By April 2nd, however, he was back in England and once more installed in his lodgings at Lambeth Palace Road.

Two days later he made the acquaintance of two pathetic creatures, Alice Marsh, aged 21, and Emma Shrivell, only 18. They had arrived from Brighton three weeks earlier and taken a room each at 118 Stamford Street, Blackfriars, a depressing thoroughfare near the Thames.

On the night of April 11th, Cream went to the girl's home, where he, Alice and Emma had an unappetising meal of tinned salmon and bottled beer. Cream pretended to sympathise with the poor girls' predicaments.

"I can do you a favour," he said, giving them three of the death-dealing capsules he always carried with him. "Take these and you won't have to worry."

"Honest? Oh thanks!" they chorused, then swallowed the poison.

"Well, it's 11 o'clock and I have to go now," Cream said abruptly, reaching for his top hat.

"I'll see you out," said Emma. And they trooped down the narrow, rickety stairs to the door.

As Emma said goodnight on the doorstep, P.C. George Cumley was passing. A Stamford Street girl seeing a man off the premises was no novelty. Nevertheless, Cumley took a good look at the tall, top-hatted, bushy-moustached, cross-eyed man who walked out of Number 118 and disappeared into the darkness.

In the wee small hours of the morning, the curtains rose on a drama similar to the earlier death scenes of Matilda Clover and Ellen Donworth. Charlotte Vogt, the girls' landlady, was jerked out of her sleep by the sound of wild screaming. She leapt out of bed and rushed to her door. When she opened it, she nearly fell over young Alice Marsh. The girl, wearing only a nightdress, was writhing in agony on the floor of the corridor.

Mrs Vogt was shocked into momentary immobility. But then another scream - from upstairs - rent the night.

"Alice!" shrieked Emma Shrivell.

Mrs Vogt rushed downstairs to call the police and a cab. Half the neighbourhood had now been roused by the tumult and were standing sleepy-eyed and white-faced at their doors. Emma Shrivell and Alice Marsh were carried into the cab and driven to St. Thomas's Hospital. Both of them were dead within the hour.

The remains of their last meal was examined and found to be free of all contamination. Subsequently, however, a post-mortem showed that strychnine had killed them both.

At breakfast on the following Sunday, Dr Cream read

newspaper reports of the girls' deaths. Later that day, Emily Sleaper, the landlady's daughter, was surprised to find him alone in the room of Walter Joseph Harper, the medical student son of a doctor. She was even more surprised when Cream began to question her closely about young Harper's background. And she was utterly flabbergasted when Cream, after opening the door and peering out to make sure no one else was listening, made his extraordinary announcement.

"You heard about those two girls being poisoned?" he asked.

"Yes, doctor," she replied. "A dreadful business."

"It was indeed. And the man who killed them was... Mr Harper!"

"You're not serious, doctor?"

"I am. He's the murderer all right. The police have the proof."

"Doctor, you're mad to say such a thing." Miss Sleaper's remark was more accurate than she knew.

Yet Cream's nosing into Harper's background had not been pointless. For, on April 26th, Dr Harper of Barnstaple, young Harper's father, received a letter accusing his son of having murdered Alice Marsh and Emma Shrivell. The writer was willing to hand over the proof - at a price. Dr Harper decided to get in touch with his son.

In the meantime Dr Cream dashed off to Berkhamstead and asked his trusting wife to write three letters, signed in the name of William H. Murray.

The first was to the two deceased girls, warning them against Harper, saying he "would serve them as he had served Matilda Clover..." The others were addressed to the coroner and to the foreman of the jury at the inquest of Marsh and Shrivell and accused William Harper of the crime.

Cream was rapidly disintegrating. His diseased brain was becoming wilder and wilder still. He began to boast of his familiarity with murders. He revealed far more than he should have known, on one occasion even providing a conducted tour of the murder spots. And, on May 12th, perhaps more by luck than judgement, he was picked up and arrested.

At his trial at the Old Bailey in October 1892, the verdict was a foregone conclusion. The evidence against him was monumental. Nonetheless, there was a moment when he thought his luck had returned. His counsel's final address to the jury was so masterly and eloquent that, when Cream returned to his remand cell that evening, he danced and sang with joy. It was a short-lived celebration, however, for the judge's summing-up the next day was deadly. The jury required only 10 minutes of deliberation to bring in a verdict of guilty.

The story of Dr Thomas Neill Cream closed on November 15th, 1892 when he was hanged at Newgate Prison. He never did confess to his crimes, but on the scaffold was alleged to have said, "I am Jack ..." just as the bolt was drawn. Doubtless his deceased mind might ever have believed he really was Jack the Ripper.

35

THE ENIGMA OF
GEORGE CHAPMAN

Not a great deal is known about the early life of George Chapman, the man whom many suspect was Jack the Ripper. We know that he was born in Poland on December 14th, 1865 and that his real name was Severin Klosowski. We know also that, as quite a young man, he found himself working as an assistant-surgeon in a hospital in Prague. And we know when he came to England: 1888, the year of the Ripper's reign of terror.

Whitechapel was then a melting-pot of immigrants and George Chapman didn't have much trouble establishing himself. Though his command of English was poor, he soon found himself work in a barber's shop in the High Street.

Chapman already had a wife in Poland but he went through a form of marriage with another Polish woman, Lucy Baderski, in London in 1889. For a time they lived together in Cable Street, and when his real wife arrived she didn't seem to object. Indeed, they formed a merry threesome or, if you included the two children, a pentad. But, it didn't last. Soon enough his wife moved out, taking the boys with her.

Shortly after this, Chapman and Lucy travelled to America where George Chapman opened his own barber's shop in Jersey City. Life in America didn't agree with Miss Baderski for she returned to London after a few months. But

Chapman lingered on until early 1892. Back in London, and once more working as a barber in the East End, Chapman tried to restore his friendship with Lucy, but his numerous other mistresses soon made that impossible. A year later he met another woman, and she became the light of his life instead. So devoted was he to Annie Chapman that he even took her name. But she left him too, after a year, tired of all his philandering.

While working in Leytonstone in 1895, Chapman met his first known victim, Mary Spink. She was married to a railway porter, but he had left her because of her excessive drinking. Chapman took his place and, following persistent badgering by her relatives, even went through a form of marriage ceremony with her. From October 1895 they lived as man and wife.

Mary Spink had private means. Her grandfather had left her £600 in trust, and Chapman used the money to buy his own hairdressing salon in Hastings in 1897. His wife worked there too, initially shaving the customers as well, which was quite a novelty at the time. Later she swapped the razor for the piano, and serenaded the salon's clients whilst her husband worked. These "musical shaves" were a popular innovation but not popular enough, alas, to keep the business going. Within six months it had closed.

The couple subsequently returned to London where Chapman decided to change careers and became the landlord of the Prince of Wales Tavern in Bartholomew Square. It was here where Mary Spink's health began to fail. Vomiting attacks and severe diarrhoea became frequent and they were helped neither by medicine nor by the glasses of brandy that Chapman tenderly brought her. She died on Christmas Day, 1897.

It was tragedy, of course. But not such a tragedy that the Prince of Wales closed its doors. Nor was it bad enough for Chapman to think twice about advertising for a replacement barmaid. By the following March, not only was a new woman serving behind the bar but Bessie Taylor had even gone through a marriage ceremony with the landlord. What was more, she, just like her predecessor, was beginning to waste away.

Several doctors were called in, but all were baffled by her constant vomiting. A Dr Stoker had some success with her case. After treating her, he arrived back at the pub to find Bessie sitting up and playing the piano. "Capital!" he cried, and went away as pleased as punch with his patent's recovery. Two days later, however, Bessie was near to death. On February 13th, 1901, she finally succumbed. Dr Stoker signed the death certificate, attributing death to "exhaustion from vomiting and diarrhoea." Bessie was duly buried at Lymm, in Cheshire, aged 36.

In August 1901, Chapman, now installed at the Monument Tavern in Union Street, spotted an advertisement in a newspaper placed by a young lady named Maud Marsh, aged 19, who was seeking a position as a barmaid. Chapman contacted her and engaged her on the spot.

Maud was an innocent girl and had little idea what terrors the world had to offer. But it wasn't long before her eyes were opened. Within weeks she was secretly writing to her mother:

"Mr has gone out, so I now write this to you to say that George says if I do not let him have what he wants he will give me £35 and send me home. What shall I do?"

Maud's mother, naturally anxious about their daughter, visited her at the Monument Tavern where Maud told them that Chapman had been "paying her attentions" and had proposed marriage. Chapman, for his part, did his best to allay their fears and assured them that his intentions were honourable. Shortly afterwards a gold band appeared on Maud Marsh's finger.

It was in early 1902 that Maud began to sicken, suffering the same symptoms as her two predecessors. A short stay in Guy's hospital led to a brief recovery, but she fell ill again when she returned home.

The same Dr Stoker who had treated Bessie Taylor was now called in to attend to her replacement. He did not seem to think it odd that two of Chapman's wives should display the same symptoms and prescribed the usual course of treatment and liquid nourishment. But Maud continued to fail rapidly. Mrs Marsh was deeply alarmed by the news and came up to sit by her daughter's bedside. She had never liked her son-in-law and she was sure this was something of his doing.

As the days passed and Maud got no better Mrs Marsh contacted her own doctor, Dr Grapel of Croydon, and told him of her suspicions. He came to visit the patient and concluded, almost immediately, that Mrs Marsh's suspicions were right and her daughter was being poisoned. However, he could not identify the poison that was being used and could not directly accuse the husband for fear of legal action of slander if proved wrong.

He took the train back to Croydon and, by this time, he had resolved what to do. He sent a telegram to Dr Stoker, telling him to look out for poison. Arsenic seemed the most likely suspect. Alas, the telegram arrived too late. Maud was already dead.

But Dr Stoker was sufficiently alarmed by his colleague's warnings that he refused to sign the death certificate. "I cannot find out what is the cause of death." he said. "It was exhaustion caused by inflammation of the bowels," Chapman told him. "What caused the inflammation?" the doctor asked. "Continual vomiting and diarrhoea?" Chapman replied. "But what caused the vomiting and diarrhoea?" the doctor persisted. There was no reply.

Dr Stoker took the brave and unusual step of conducting a private autopsy, without informing the coroner. He discovered what he took to be arsenic in the remains, and then wrote to the coroner, Dr Waldo, and also informed the police.

Chapman was arrested on the morning of Saturday, October 25th, 1902. Police searched his premises and found many documents, medicines and powders and almost £300 in gold and notes. For the first time they realised that the prisoner's real name was Severin Klosowski. That evening Chapman/Klosowski was charged under both his names with the murder of Maud Marsh,

The trial of George Chapman began at the Old Bailey on March 16th, 1903.

When he appeared in court, Chapman looked pale. Defeated even. And, perhaps that was wise. The facts were so damning that it was impossible to see how any counsel, judge or jury could have failed to convict him. It would have been pointless to hang on to any hope, and he duly went to the gallows on April 7th, 1903.

There was one curious aspect about the case, one thing that could have saved him: Chapman had no motive. He was an accomplished seducer, a real Casanova. Why should he kill women when he could love them and leave them so easily. He did not kill for money, since he had insured none of his victims. And he was not legally married to any of his three known victims, so they had no claim against him. So why did he do it?

This enigma proved no problem for the prosecutor. Solicitor General, Sir Edward Carson, had boldly declared his views in court: "Learned counsel for the defence has commented upon the absence of motive," he announced. "But what is the use of seeking for motive when we have the actual fact of murder? In this instance there was the most ample motive, for the prisoner's was a history of unbridled, heartless and cruel lust."

Was this, then, the reason? Was it just "cruel lust" that had brought an end to these three women's lives. And, if it was, why was this lust just limited to three. Were there, perhaps, more victims elsewhere?

Certainly, one man thought so. Chief Inspector Abberline, who headed the inquiries into the Jack the Ripper murder, was convinced that George Chapman was his killer too. When Chapman was arrested, Abberline told the arresting officers, "I see you have caught Jack the Ripper at last!" Thirty years later, in his book, *Forty Years of Manhunting*, Inspector Neil also shared this opinion. "We were never able to secure proof that Chapman was the Ripper," he wrote, but "it is the most fitting and sensible solution to the possible identity of the murderer."

To most observers, it hardly seems likely that a vicious mutilator like Jack the Ripper would have changed his method of killing to the comparatively gentle administering of poison. But it is not beyond the bounds of possibility.

Being apprenticed to a surgeon in Poland for six years, Chapman certainly had the necessary anatomical skill to have removed organs and mutilate bodies in the manner of the Ripper killings. He arrived in London from Poland in 1988 and lived and worked in Whitechapel just when the murders began and left shortly after they ended. Chapman's physical description fits that of the man seen with the last of the Ripper's victims and the American-style phrases used in the Ripper's letter would also have fitted Chapman.

Chapman did go to America in May 1890, and, it is said, a series of Ripper-type murders then occurred in the locality of Jersey City, ceasing only when Chapman returned to London in May 1892.

It is also a curious coincidence that one of Chapman's mistresses should have been named Annie Chapman, the same name as that of the Ripper's second victim.

So was Chapman the Ripper? We will never know because he was executed on April 7th 1903.

36

THE MONKEY MAN

Charles Peace's early career as a criminal was none too promising. Jailed at 19 for receiving stolen property, he went on to spend seventeen of his next twenty-one years behind bars or suffering hard labour. But, on August 9th, 1872, he arrived home to greet his wife and children, and vowed he would never return to jail again. True to his word, he never did.

Charlie was an able villain. Although permanently disabled, following an injury as a child, he possessed remarkable agility. He could scale walls and climb drainpipes like no one else in the country and, from 1872 onwards, he used these talents with a vengeance. No more did he indulge in the foolishness of old. There were no more stupid mistakes, like when he was apprehended while drunk in the house he was burgling. No more boasting about his exploits and no more associating with other villains. Charlie was now the consummate professional.

By day Charles Peace lived as a respectable Sheffield family man. His children went to Sunday School and he and his wife attended church. By night, however, he was one of the most successful cat burglars the country had ever known.

He always "cased" his targets beforehand, looking not only for an access, but for escape routes if needed. Then, often disguised, he would creep in noiselessly, disturbing no one. Charlie worked with such speed and stealth that sleeping occupants never awoke - not even when he slid his hand beneath their pillows to snatch their wallets.

For years he carried on like this, burgling as many as six homes every night, and still he was never caught. But then, in 1875 Charles Peace met his nemesis - a woman by the name of Catherine Dyson.

Charlie had always played fast and loose with the affections of women and, when Mr and Mrs Dyson moved into a house a few doors away from his, it was inevitable that she too would become the object of his flirtatious attentions. This time, however, flirtation was only the start of things. Soon it had developed into an insane, uncontrollable passion. Alas, it was a passion that Catherine Dyson did not share.

But Charles Peace refused to be put off. He dogged Catherine constantly, never allowing her or her husband a moment's privacy or rest. He proclaimed his love, he sent her letters, he kept watch on her house day and night. Finally, when still she said "No," Charlie Peace cracked. On July 1st, 1876, he accosted Catherine Dyson in the street and brandished a revolver in her face. "I will blow your bloody brains out - and your husband's brains out too."

Next day, the Dysons lodged a complaint at the local magistrates' court, and obtained a summons against their difficult neighbour. As a convicted criminal, the last thing Peace wanted was the police taking an interest in him, and so, before things got more difficult still, he chose to admit defeat. He packed up all his belongings and, with his wife and family, departed for a new address in Hull.

But Charlie's infatuation for Catherine didn't dim. Soon he found himself, once more, outside the Dysons' door, peering in at his beloved through the window. The Dysons despaired. It was now clear that the only way to escape their daily harassment was to move house. In due course, therefore, they installed themselves at a new residence on the other side of Sheffield. Yet, even this did no good. The following evening the Dysons found Charlie skulking on their doorstep. "I care nought for the warrants, nor the bobbies," he declared, "I will follow you wherever you go."

A little after 8 o'clock on the evening of November 29th, Catherine Dyson, a lantern in her hand, walked across her back yard to use the communal privy. There, in the shadows, was Charlie Peace, a revolver in his hand. Catherine screamed and her husband dashed out to help her. Charlie raised his gun and shot the man straight through the temple.

Charlie Peace was now a wanted killer. Posters were circulated nationally. They read: "MURDER - ONE HUNDRED POUNDS REWARD." And yet they did little good. It wasn't until two years later that Charlie was finally caught.

On October 10th, 1878, he was in London, living under the alias of John Ward. A large house in St John's Park, Blackheath had caught his eye as a good target for robbery and, with his usual care and attention, he had just begun to break in. At that very moment, however, P.C. Robinson had walked down the road. Spying the burglar, he ran across to grab him. Peace pulled out his gun, but the burly police constable overpowered him, battering Peace over the head with the butt of the revolver.

It took a while for the police to realise that the criminal that they had in their charge was a man wanted for murder. But, eventually, the identification was made and, on January 17th, 1879, Charlie Peace was taken by train to Sheffield to appear in court for the murder of Arthur Dyson. On the journey he made a dramatic attempt to escape by throwing himself, handcuffed, out of the carriage window. But it was to no avail. He succeeded only in cracking his head. The case went ahead and Charlie Peace was found guilty.

Charlie spent most of his last days in prayer. Though he had pleaded his innocence during the trial, he now readily confessed. Moreover, he also confessed to the murder of

P.C. Nicholas Cook at Whalley Range, Manchester in August 1876.

On the day of his execution, Peace asked if he might speak to his executioner William Marwood. It was an unprecedented request and one that has never since been repeated. But it was granted.

It is not known what passed between the two men but, for over a quarter of an hour, they sat talking together. Then, as the time of the execution approached, the door of the condemned cell opened and Peace and Marwood stood to leave.

"I hope you will not punish me. I hope you will do your work quickly," Peace requested. "You will not suffer pain from my hand," the hangman replied.

Charles Peace grasped Marwood's arm "God bless you. I hope to meet you all in Heaven. I am thankful my sins are all forgiven," he said.

Then began the long open-air walk to the gallows. As Charlie reached the scaffold he began to pray.

Gently, almost tenderly, William Marwood placed the cap over his head, then adjusted the rope around his neck. In mid-prayer, Charlie was launched through the trap into eternity.

Charles had written his own memorial card: "In memory of Charles Peace who was executed in Armley Prison Tuesday February 25th 1879. Aged 47. For that I don but never intended."

37

THE BODY SNATCHERS

It was an act of kindness that prompted Mr and Mrs Hare to invite William Burke and Helen McDougal to stay at their home. With the harvest over, they had intended to travel to the west of Scotland and find more work. But Maggie Hare insisted. "Irishmen should stick together," she said. "Anyway," she went on, "it makes good sense." Staying with them in Edinburgh would mean few expenses, she explained, and it would give William an excellent opening for carrying on business as a cobbler.

It didn't take long for Burke and his mistress to be convinced. Soon afterwards the four of them were travelling to the Hare's lodging house, in Tanner's Close in Edinburgh's West Port. The die was cast for Burke and Hare's reign of brutal butchery.

It was about three months later, just before Christmas, 1827, when the careers that would bring such infamy on the two men began.

A lodger in the Hare's home, an army pensioner by the name of Donald, had the misfortune to die whilst still owing his landlord £4. It caused Hare considerable distress. He thought, not unreasonably, that any money Donald might have, would now be sent to a relation. The rent due to him would thus never be paid. "Why should that be?" he complained. But he couldn't see any way to avoid the loss. And then he had an idea.

"Donald's body is not much use to him at present," he reasoned, "but it is a good deal of use to me."

Off he went and found Burke to tell him his plan. He explained, as there was really no prospect of ever getting his £4 from Donald's relations, he proposed to take the body out of the coffin and sell it to one of the schools of anatomy in the city.

At first, Burke was shocked. But times were so hard that he agreed. If the matter could be arranged without risk, it was well worth trying. The pair returned at once to Tanner's Close and, unscrewing the coffin lid, removed all that remained of the old man. They replaced his body with a sack of bark and stones, then refastened the lid in place. Donald's corpse was still under his bed when the coffin was taken to the cemetery and solemnly buried.

That evening Burke and Hare went to Surgeons' Square with a view to making arrangements for the selling of the body. Hare, always cunning but something of a coward, would go no further than the corner of the square. But Burke marched right up to the door of the celebrated Anatomy School. There he waited until he was noticed by one of the students.

"Are you Dr Knox?" Burke asked.

"No," answered the student, "but I am one of his assistants."

"Perhaps you may do as well," continued Burke, but he could not bring himself to explain the precise nature of his business.

He needn't have worried. The student was an old hand at dealing with body-snatchers and had no time for pleasantries. He asked him outright where the thing was. Burke professed not to understand him and so he was taken into the dissecting-room where he saw the remains of various subjects lying on tables. Burke now explained that he had got a corpse for sale and asked what the remuneration usually was.

"Ten pounds," said the student, "Sometimes more, sometimes less. It depends on the body."

"And would you not give a pound or two for a fresh one?" asked Burke.

The student who was making the deal ignored the question but told Burke that the body would have be seen before a price could be agreed. He said that the body should be brought to the dissecting rooms at 10 o'clock that night. To this Burke readily agreed and hurried out of the building to rejoin his companion.

It was in high spirits that the two men went back to Tanner's Close. Packing Donald's body into a sack, they merrily hauled it back to Dr Knox's establishment. They were a little disappointed with Knox's valuation. He said it was worth only £7.10s. But they agreed to his price.

Once outside, Burke and Hare rejoiced at the ease with which their money had been made. They talked of nothing else on their way home and it wasn't long before Burke got the notion of repeating the exercise and making it more profitable still. In order to get the best rate, he said, they could manufacture the bodies themselves. This dreadful suggestion did not horrify Hare in the least. He readily entered into the scheme. So too did the two women, Helen McDougal and Mrs Hare.

It was on February 11th, 1828 that Hare met the first victim of their new enterprise. She was an old woman by the name of Abigail Simpson. She came from a little village some miles outside the city but had come into Edinburgh to visit the Grassmarket.

Hare approached her, pretending that he had met her before and, under the influence of drink she entered into eager conversation with him. When he suggested that she should come to his house, she readily agreed.

Mrs Hare made much of the old lady and plied her with drink. Soon Abigail was far too drunk to go home and Hare suggested that she stop the night. This plan she gladly fell in with and lay down to sleep off the effects of her friends' hospitality.

For the greater part of the night Burke and Hare watched over her, but they were unable to do the deed. They had contemplated murder often enough, but actually committing the crime was far more daunting than they had imagined. They just couldn't go through with it. Morning came, Abigail awoke and the two men stared at each other shamefaced. But they had gone so far, they couldn't back out now.

Abigail was still weak from the whisky, so all was not yet lost. Expressing great concern that she should restore her strength, the couple proposed that she should have a little whisky and porter, as a corrective. The concoction did its work only too well. In a short time the old woman was more intoxicated than ever.

Then the moment arrived. Hare placed his hand over Abigail's mouth and nostrils to stop her breathing, while Burke laid himself across her body to prevent any struggling or disturbance. The poor old soul was far too feeble and drunk to make any resistance. A few minutes was all that was needed for the fiendish work to be over.

With Mrs Simpson finally dead, her murderers instantly stripped her body and concealed it in a box they had prepared in advance. The woman's clothes were tied up in a bundle with some stones and sunk in the canal.

Later that day, Hare went to Dr Knox's room, where Abigail's body was valued at £10. Dr Knox approved of the freshness of his purchase and asked no questions. The Burke and Hare business had begun.

Two more old women had taken the short cut to Dr Knox's slab when, on April 8th, Burke bumped into Mary Paterson and her friend Janet Brown in Swanston's liquor store. Both girls were 18 and both were prostitutes. Mary, the more attractive of the two, was well-known among Edinburgh's students for the voluptuousness of her body.

Burke inveigled the two girls into his brother's house in Gibb's Close, where they emptied two bottles of whisky. Mary was the first to pass out, and Burke was wondering how to get rid of her clearer-headed friend when things started going wrong.

Helen McDougal suddenly burst in and, seeing the two

drunken prostitutes draped round her mate, jumped to the wrong conclusion. She launched herself at the two girls in a barrage of abuse. Janet Brown fled, but Mary Paterson was too stupefied to move. Burke then explained to his mistress that the whole set-up had been a matter of business. Helen McDougal bit her lip.

Soon the ghoulish Hare was staring down at the flushed and snoring Mary Paterson. It was a pity to snuff out such a lovely creature, the two men thought. But, after all, £10 was £10.

Four hours later, the remains of Mary Paterson were safely in Dr Knox's dissecting room.

Burke and Hare became the scourge of Edinburgh, whisking innocent victims off the streets and into their tea-chest for the one-way journey to 10 Surgeons' Square. No one was safe.

One morning Burke saw two policemen dragging a drunken woman into the West Port lock-up. His humane feelings were offended at their roughness. "Let her go," he said, "I know where she lodges and I'll take her home." The policemen were only too glad to leave their incapable prisoner with a kind neighbour. That evening the ghastly tea-chest made another trip.

Emboldened by their success, Burke and Hare ranged wider for their victims and plumbed ever lower levels of callousness and brutality.

An old Irish woman, leading her 12-year old grandson by the hand, stopped Burke in the street to ask the way. Burke said he knew the address she was looking for, but suggested she refreshed herself at his home first.

While Mrs Hare and Helen McDougal looked after the boy, a deaf mute, Burke treated the woman to as much as she could drink. When she was suitably befuddled, he called Hare and they smothered her with the bedclothes.

With the old woman dead, there was now the problem of the little boy. Maggie Hare and Helen McDougal were disinclined to carry on entertaining the lad, and the danger of taking him home to his mother without a plausible explanation of what had happened to his grandmother was all too apparent.

Before the women could even begin to lament on the peril of their circumstances, Burke took the matter in hand. He led the pitiful child up to the private flat where the dead woman lay under the bedclothes and sat the boy down on his knee. Then, without warning, he jerked the young fellow backwards with such force that the boy's back was broken over his leg. Unmoved by such piteous groans of agony as the boy could make, he continued to press on the lad's chest and hips until the final crack convinced him that the spine had snapped and the poor boy was dead.

In a trice, the four ghouls had stripped both bodies. The double-load was too heavy for the customary tea-chest so the corpses were rammed into an enormous old herring barrel. Burke and Hare then got a porter to wheel the barrow to the good Dr Knox who counted out a record £16 for his catch.

When it came to business, the two Williams made no exception, even amongst kith and kin. Ann McDougal, a distant relative of Burke's, came to visit them during the summer and she too was murdered and sold. The only concession that Burke made to family feelings as they put her to death was that, this time, Hare did the stifling while he sat on her chest.

Nor were employees exempt from contributing to the Burke and Hare fortune and the medical school's resources. Ann McDougal was followed to Surgeon's Square by Burke's washer-woman, Mrs Hostler.

The frightful list grew longer and grislier. In nine months of enterprise, at least nineteen bodies were sold.

For such a ghoulish pair the end came, appropriately enough, on Halloween 1828. It was then that Burke was taking his usual shot at Rymer's liquor store and saw an old woman begging for coppers. Burke summed her up at one glance as an ideal "specimen" and the two were soon swapping reminiscences of Ireland, their common homeland.

The woman's name was Mary Docherty, and she was delighted to accompany Burke back to a "Halloween party" at his house, As soon as her hands were safely curled round a glass, Burke sought out Hare. "I've got a good shot in the house for the doctor," he said gleefully.

The two returned home with plenty of whisky; the chairs were cleared away and the macabre party began. To make more room, the revellers threw out two new lodgers, a married couple named James and Ann Gray. The fewer snoopers around the house, they thought, the better.

The sounds of their merrymaking echoed down the street. Burke and Mary Docherty danced an Irish jig, which ended abruptly when Burke trod on the woman's bare foot with his hobnailed boots. Drunken laughter alternated with bouts of brawling and quarrelling. But, just before midnight, the tone of the party changed.

Grocer Hugh Alston was on his way home past the house when he heard a woman's voice cry "Murder!" He ran to the top of the street to look for a policeman, but gave up the search when the noise from the house died down.

Early on the morning of Sunday, November 2nd, the police "acting on information received" raided 10, Surgeons' Square. They asked to see a tea-chest.

Paterson, the doorkeeper, showed them to the cellar. The chest, which had been delivered the night before, was still there, unopened. While Paterson protested, the police forced open the lid. Crammed inside, her head touching her knees, was the naked body of Mary Docherty.

Burke and Hare had been betrayed, but by whom?

On Christmas Eve, the spectators in Edinburgh's High Court sat sickened as William Hare, his face twitching, told his self-vindicating version of the last hours of Mary Docherty's life.

It seemed incredible that Hare, who had apparently sat and watched while his friend choked the life out of an old woman, should now be giving evidence for the Crown. But it was the only way the prosecution could clinch the case against Burke. Hare had snatched at the chance of skipping clear of the gallows by turning King's evidence.

The trial lasted a full 24 hours, after which the guilt of both men was well beyond doubt. The prosecution had chosen only to try the case of Miss Docherty's murder but, inevitably, the stories of the other gruesome killings also came out. No one in the court had heard of anything so ghastly before.

No sympathy was wasted on William Burke as a crowd of 25,000 defied torrential rain to watch him mount the Edinburgh gallows on January 28th, 1829. Nor did anyone spare much for the feelings of Dr Knox whose career was now in tatters. He left Edinburgh in disgrace to become a showman in a travelling group of American Indians.

So great was the feeling against Hare that he had to be protected by the police and, on several occasions, he took refuge in jail. At length he managed to get out of Scotland and obtained employment in some lime works but, one day, the labourers discovered his identity. They flung him into one of the pits. He managed to escape, but lost his eyesight, and for the remainder of his days he begged for bread.

38

JACK THE RIPPER'S LAST VICTIM

"Early on Saturday morning a ghastly murder was perpetrated near Spitalfields Market. The latest deed of ferocity has thrown Whitechapel into a state of panic... with so much cunning was the horrifying deed carried out that apparently no clue has been left. We are certainly led to imagine some baleful prowler of the East-end streets and alleys who... knows every bye-place, who is plausible enough in address to beguile his victims, strong enough to overcome them the moment homicidal passion succeeds to desire, cunning enough to select the most quiet hour and the most quiet spot for his furious assaults, and possessed of a certain ghastly skill in using the knife."

So read the Daily Telegraph on Monday, September 10th, 1888. No wonder London's East End was close to panic. The report told of the murder of Annie Chapman, who had been the latest victim of the Ripper. Within the month there would be two more. There would also be the letter from the killer:

"I am down on whores," the Ripper announced, "and shan't quit ripping them till I do get buckled (arrested)... The next job I do, I shall clip the lady's ear off. My knife is nice and sharp and I want to get to work right away, if I get the chance. Good luck, Yours truly, Jack the Ripper"

The letter was sent to the Central News Agency on September 28th and subsequently appeared in many of the papers. Whether or not it was a practical joke or a missive from the murderer himself, no one knows. But it was clearly designed to terrorise London's prostitutes, and it worked.

With no one was it more successful than with Mary Jane Kelly, a 25-year-old prostitute who lived in a tiny one-roomed flat on the ground floor of Miller's Court at 26 Dorset Street (now Duval Street).

It was not a good address. No fewer than 1,200 people were crammed in the Dorset Street's various lodging houses and brothels. Beggars, thieves and roughnecks were all around. Worse still, it was here that the Ripper liked to strike. Annie Chapman, his second victim, and Liz Stride, victim number three, both lived at 35 Dorset Street, while the fourth victim, Kate Eddowes, had dwelt for a time at number 26. Mary Ann Nichols, the first victim, lived in Thrawl Street. But that was just around the corner. Mary Jane was petrified lest she should be next.

Her partner at the time, Joseph Barnett, recalled how she would always ask him to read the newspaper reports. "If I did not bring one home, she would get it herself and ask me whether the murderer was caught."

Increasingly Mary Jane talked about returning home. To her neighbour, Lizzie Albrook, she confided that she was sick of her way of life and wished she had enough money to go back to her family in Ireland. "I don't believe she would have gone out as she did", said Lizzie, "if she had not been obliged to do so in order to keep herself from starvation. About the last thing she said to me was: 'Whatever you do, don't go wrong and turn out as I have'."

Every prostitute has a tragic tale to tell, but few are more poignant than that of Mary Jane, or Marie Jeanette as she preferred to be called, or "Ginger" as she was known, because of her near waist-length auburn hair.

It is widely believed, although sometimes disputed, that Mary Jane was born in Limerick, Ireland and though the family moved to Caernarvon when she was quite young, she still regarded Ireland as her home. Evidently her mother did too, and must have returned there, because she would frequently receive letters from her bearing an Irish postmark.

Legend has it that her family were well-educated, which was unusual for the time. But the girl did not make much use of her advantage. Against her parents' wishes she married a Welsh miner when she was 16 and, when he died in a pit fire a few years later, she became virtually destitute. She travelled to Cardiff to see a cousin who might have helped her. It was he who initiated her into the world of prostitution. "As I told her," said Barnett, "that was her downfall."

Eventually moving to London, she found work in a fashionable West End brothel, where she prospered. A brief episode followed in France with a "gentleman," and then, in 1884, Mary returned to London. This time though, fortune did not smile on her and she ended up on the wrong side of the city.

First she took up with a cockney trader named Morganstone; then came Joseph Fleming, a mason's plasterer and one of her more favoured lovers. Indeed, she remained fond of Fleming and saw him regularly, even after their relationship had ended.

Joseph Barnett was her next partner. "I picked up with her in Commercial Street," he recalled. "The first night we had a drink together. I arranged to see her the next day. And then on Saturday we agreed to remain together."

Although there were some indications to the contrary Barnett claimed that they lived happily enough together. Disputes with Mary Jane were over quickly and would be followed by days and sometimes weeks of peace. "Often, I brought her things coming home," he said. "And whatever it was, she always liked it." But after Barnett lost his job things became difficult. Perhaps because they didn't have money for the rent that the couple moved house so frequently. From George Street they moved to Paternoster Court, then to Dorset Street and after that to Brick Lane before returning to Dorset Street and their current abode. And their relationship suffered as a result.

There were now many fights and arguments between them, usually concerning Mary Jane's behaviour and occupation. According to Barnett she had grown increasingly wild and increasingly active.

A neighbour said that, when she was sober, Mary Jane was "one of the most decent and nicest girls you could meet." Under the influence, however, she was a loud, boisterous and belligerent drunk. As her landlord, John McCarthy put it, Mary was normally "an exceptionally quiet woman, but when in drink, she had more to say." Joseph Barnett began to find her hard to endure and when, one drunken evening at the end of October, she went so far as to bring home two fellow prostitutes to share their bed, he decided enough was enough. They had a furious row. Things were thrown, windows were broken and Barnett moved out.

He continued to call, however, almost every day. He even said he might move back in with her. But he never did. Maybe she didn't want him. Her friend, Julia Venturney, certainly didn't think she did. Mary Jane "could not bear the man Joe she was living with, although he was very good to her," she said. Also, as it later transpired, Mary Jane was pregnant. Did Joseph know she was expecting? Did she think he was the father? Was she planning an abortion? Did Joseph know she was expectant? It's anybody's guess. Today we just don't know.

What we do know, however, is that Joseph visited Mary Jane in the early evening of November 8th and, as soon as he had gone, she went out and got drunk. One woman told of seeing her inebriated that night. Another told of her accompanying an unknown man, short and fat with a carroty moustache. Yet another spoke of her being with a well dressed gentleman who had a large gold chain across his waistcoat and a distinctive gold horseshoe pin in his tie. Many recalled hearing her singing. Sweet Violets was the song she performed.

According to most reports, Mary Ann stumbled back to Miller's Court at 1.30 in the morning, or a little after. She was alone, though there may have been a man outside watching. She went into her room and shut the door.

It was at around 10.45 when Thomas Bowyer, the landlord's assistant, came over to Miller's Court to collect Mary Jane's rent. He knocked on the door, but got no reply. Reluctant to return empty handed, at 35 shillings the rent owing was quite considerable, he knocked again. Still getting no response, he lifted himself up at the side of the door and peered through a broken window.

There, in a welter of blood, was the butchered corpse of Mary Jane Kelly.

It had been more than a month since the Ripper's last attack, but he had made up for it now. The attack was even more frenzied than usual. Every inch of the room was covered with blood and flesh. Mary Jane's entrails were draped over a picture frame and her heart was placed on the pillow of her bed. Her breasts, her nose, her thighs and her legs, had been put on the table.

Though there was a candle in the room, it had not been used. Jack had apparently worked by the light of a pile of rags, the ashes of which were burnt in the grate. It must have taken him all night. So grisly was his dissection that it took morticians six hours to piece her remains together. Before then Joseph Barnett had to identify the body - only her hair and her eyes were available for him to see.

The following description of the mutilations was published in the Illustrated Police News:

"The throat had been cut right across with a knife, nearly severing the head from the body. The abdomen had been partially ripped open, and both of the breasts had been cut from the body, the left arm, like the head, hung to the body by the skin only. The nose had been cut off, the forehead skinned, and the thighs, down to the feet, stripped of the flesh, The abdomen had been slashed with a knife across and downwards, and the liver and entrails wrenched away. The entrails and other portions of the frame were missing, but the liver, etc., it is said, were found placed between the feet of this poor victim. The flesh from the thighs and legs, together with the breasts and nose, had been placed by the murderer on the table, and one of the hands of the dead woman had been pushed into her stomach"

It was the worst killing of the Ripper's reign. It was also the last. After Mary Jane's slaughter, the murders abruptly stopped. No one knows why.

Mary Jane Kelly was later buried at Leytonstone Cemetery. Before she was interred the police photographed both of her eyes. They hoped that her retinas might somehow have retained an image of her killer. The experiment, however, was unsuccessful. The identity of Jack the Ripper remained unknown.

39

THE EVIL PRITCHARD

Edward William Pritchard scraped a medical degree by the slimmest of margins, and spent the early part of his career as an undistinguished naval surgeon. But he struck gold when he met and married Mary Jane Taylor, the daughter of a rich Edinburgh silk merchant.

In the spring of 1850, after a year of wedlock, he resigned his commission to take up private practice in Hunmanby, Yorkshire. Needless to say, this was made possible thanks to the generosity of his wife's rich parents. It was an arrangement that Pritchard made the most of.

Dr Pritchard's bedside manner and charm outweighed the more formal demands of medical ability and he used them both to assure his success. Adored by his female patients he soon outgrew his first practice and moved to a larger concern in nearby Filey. But now his indiscretions were beginning to catch up with him. He had to flee his new home shortly afterwards, dragging his long suffering wife in tow and leaving behind an angry group of husbands.

The Pritchards now moved to Glasgow, where they lived at 11 Berkeley Terrace. It was here that the doctor committed his first murder.

Pritchard had begun an affair with a young servant and, when he and the girl were alone in the house, a fire broke out in her room and she was burned to death. All the evidence pointed to the girl being drugged, after which her room had been deliberately set ablaze. But no inquiries were made, despite some pointed remarks in the press.

After the fire, the Pritchards decided to move again, to 22, Royal Crescent, Glasgow. To replace the maid he had murdered, Pritchard engaged a local girl named Mary McLeod. Though she was only fifteen, he found her rather attractive and he seduced her after she had been in the house only a few days. From then on, there was rarely a night when she slept alone.

Almost exactly a year later, in the spring of 1864, the Pritchards moved yet once more, this time to Clarence Place.

It was here, in November, that Mrs Pritchard started to become ill. She was constantly in bed with general weakness and attacks of vomiting. "I must have caught a chill," she said innocently. Neither she nor anyone else thought it odd that she recovered whenever she went to stay with her parents in Edinburgh, only to fall ill as soon as she returned home to the doctor.

During the following January, Mrs Pritchard became much worse with severe bouts of vomiting after meals. But it was hardly surprising. Dr Pritchard was lacing his wife's food and drink with large doses of antimony and aconite.

Playing the part of the worried husband, Pritchard contacted Dr James Cowan, one of his wife's relations, but prudently cut down the doses of poison he was giving before the doctor called. Dr Cowan therefore saw little to be concerned about. "I don't think there is anything seriously wrong with her," he declared, "I recommend mustard poultices, and champagne and ice for nourishment."

Two hours after Dr Cowan's departure, however, Mrs Pritchard had another serious attack.

On February 10th, 1865, Mrs Taylor, Mrs Pritchard's mother, left Edinburgh for Glasgow to help her sick daughter run the household. The indomitable 70-year-old woman was shocked to see how ill her daughter was, and she installed herself in Mary's bedroom. Dr Pritchard quickly realised that he would have to get her out of the way too.

A few days later, Mrs Pritchard was given some tapioca, but before she ate it Mrs Taylor sampled the dish and, as a consequence, was violently sick. "I must have caught the same complaint as my daughter," she said. The poor woman had no idea how grimly accurate her remark had been.

One afternoon, Mrs Taylor left her daughter's bedside to have her tea downstairs. A few minutes later she returned to the bedroom racked by violent spasms as she vainly tried to vomit. Exhausted by these tremendous efforts and the effects of the poison that had been in her tea, she was soon unconscious.

Later that night, Dr Pritchard sent for a local physician, a Dr Paterson, to see what he could do. He came as soon as he could and was immediately directed to Mary Pritchard's bedroom. As he opened the door he was confronted with a scene like something from a modern horror film. In the close, stuffy atmosphere of the lamp-lit bedroom, Mrs Taylor lay fully-clothed on the bed, breathing heavily in a coma caused by poison and exhaustion. Then Paterson saw that she was not alone. There was also another woman in the bed. It was the dying Mrs Pritchard, her dull eyes wide with horror in a deathly pale, wasted face. Her appearance was so strikingly typical that Dr Paterson told himself: "My God! She's suffering from antimony poisoning."

As for Mrs Taylor, Dr Paterson said that her case was hopeless. His judgement was sound, for she died early the next day.

Dr Paterson now found himself in an awkward situation. If he went to the authorities with an accusation, his position would be absolutely untenable if he were subsequently proved wrong. And even if Dr Pritchard had been poisoning his wife, one hint of suspicion and he could stop. Mrs Pritchard would recover, and then Dr Paterson would face a crippling suit for slander.

Fortunately for Dr Paterson's peace of mind, temporarily at least, he was offered a way out. He was asked to sign

Mrs Taylor's death certificate and refused. He sent a strong letter to the Registrar saying that he could not sign the document and gave a good indication as to why. But the Registrar failed to see the plain implication of the letter, and ordered no enquiry or post-mortem. The road was clear for Dr Pritchard to continue the slow, cruel slaughter of his wife. And now he was even more reckless than before.

On Monday, March 13th, the doctor sent some cheese up to his wife. Mary McLeod tasted a piece, and immediately had a burning sensation in her throat together with a terrible thirst. The very next morning, the cook, Mary Patterson, ate a piece and experienced the same symptoms. She was so ill that she had to go to bed for the rest of the day.

The following morning, Dr Pritchard helped to make an egg-flip for his wife. The cook tasted the drink.

"Ugh! It's horrible!" she spluttered.

"You're just not used to the taste," Dr Pritchard replied smoothly. Turning to Mary McLeod he said: "Here, Mary, take this up to your mistress."

Mrs Pritchard drank some of the egg-flip. It made her violently sick.

At 5 p.m. on Friday, March 17th, 1865, Dr Pritchard gave his wife another drink. Almost immediately she was seized by a violent attack of cramp. Dr Paterson was called in again, and he prescribed a sleeping draught.

As soon as he had gone, Dr Pritchard got into bed beside his wife, while Mary McLeod lay on a couch in the same room.

At 1 a.m., Dr Pritchard sent the girl to prepare a mustard poultice. Alone with his wife, the doctor looked at her prostrate form. For months her frail body had somehow resisted all the onslaughts of antimony and aconite; the slender threads of life had refused to snap. Until now he had carefully hidden his impatience but now the doctor could stand it no longer.

He reached for the chloroform bottle and pad which were kept near the bed for the moments when Mrs

Pritchard's pain was too agonizing to bear. He pressed the pad over his wife's unconscious face and left it there until her last breath was stilled.

Mary McLeod, carrying the poultice, returned to the bedroom with the cook, Mary Patterson. The two women realized almost at once that Mrs Pritchard was dead. Play-acting like a fifth-rate touring actor, Dr Pritchard sobbed: "Come back! Come back! My dear Mary Jane, don't leave your dear Edward!"

On the following Monday, Dr Pritchard took the body to Edinburgh. There, in the presence of his in-laws, he had the lid taken off the coffin. With tears in his eyes, the murderer kissed his victim on the lips.

Meanwhile, back in Glasgow, someone had written an anonymous letter to the police. Dr Paterson subsequently denied that he was the author, but it could only have been written by someone qualified to diagnose the reasons for Mrs Pritchard's death.

The police moved swiftly. They took bedclothes and bottles from the house. They also learned that Dr Pritchard had purchased large quantities of aconite and antimony over the past few months. When the doctor returned to Glasgow, he was met at the railway station by a police reception committee, which took him straight to jail.

Yet, Mrs Pritchard's relatives and the members of the doctor's household continued to believe him innocent. Only when his wife's body was exhumed and found to contain a fatal dose of poison, did their opinions begin to change.

Dr Edward William Pritchard came to trial on July 3rd, 1865, less than two months after the death of his wife. To begin with he made an excellent impression. One report said of him:

"He is rather a good-looking fellow, with clearly defined features, and a beard much to be admired. He looked the most cool and unconcerned person in the court." And another declared:

"The prisoner is a tall, well-built man, rather prepossessing. The impression conveyed is one of mildness. His face during the day was sad and thoughtful." But, as the prosecution continued to hammer away, the façade began to crack. Although no motive could be suggested for the murders, by the end of the trial the jury needed only an hour to decide to send Dr Pritchard to the gallows.

While awaiting execution, the doctor finally confessed to the killings.

On July 28th, 1865, Dr Edward William Pritchard was hanged before 100,000 people. He was the last criminal to be publicly executed in Scotland.

40

THE EASTWOOD POISONINGS

Sarah was a striking sight. Living in the Nottinghamshire
town of Eastwood, later the birthplace of D.H. Lawrence,
she towered above almost everyone else in the town. She
stood six feet two inches in her stockinged feed and, always
conscious that her otherwise slender build made her look
freakish, she wore at least 12 petticoats to balance things
out.

She looked positively Amazonian, and yet there was
nothing ungainly about her. As a teenager she had excelled
at all sports, and she had a good figure. She was described
as being fair-haired and quite attractive. She certainly had
her full share of admirers.

For the very beginning, however, Sarah had been an
unlucky girl. Her father had died before she was born and
her mother followed him two years later. Her grandmother
looked after her for a while, but then she too died. Then, to
cap it all, at the age of 15, she had the misfortune to meet
Joseph Barber.

Barber was a horse dealer and a rascal. He was 28 at the
time, and it was said that there wasn't a good-looking
woman in Eastwood whom he hadn't already bedded, plus
a few ugly ones too, when the nights were dark and he was
full of ale.

As soon as he discovered that Sarah had been left £1,000
by her grandparents, he bedded her too. And two years

later, when she was just 17, they were married.

It was a most unhappy union. Barber was vicious and violent. When he was drunk, which was often enough, he would beat her unmercifully. More than once he was seen chasing his wife down the street, thrashing her with a stick. He quickly disposed of most of his wife's inheritance on wild living, and continued to pursue almost every woman in sight.

By the time she was twenty, Sarah had had enough. She went to France with a lover of her own, a man named Gillott, and they settled in Paris. Soon enough, however, she found that her lover was not much better than her husband. Once the honeymoon period was over, Gillott's main interest in life appeared to be that of securing her purse - something that Sarah had no intention of giving up. As soon as he realised this, Gillott deserted her and returned to England.

Sarah remained in Paris for a few months, living a somewhat solitary life. And it was here that, out of the blue, Joe Barber suddenly appeared at her door. With proverbial cap in hand, Sarah's husband begged her to give him one more chance. If she came back home to him, he declared, he would give up all his bad ways. On bended knee, he vowed that the days of drink and wild women were over. He would settle down and become a respectable married man.

It was like expecting a leopard to shed its spots, but Sarah did return and, for at least a week, Barber kept his promise. But then the drink, the women and the violence began as before, Only now things had changed. Sarah was no longer afraid of him. Barber might scare the men of Eastwood with his all too ready fists, but he could no longer frighten his wife. She would meet him head-on and give as good as she got.

The months went by, so did the years, and, against all probabilities, the unlikely couple stayed together. There were arguments of course, and many fights, yet Sarah and Joseph seemed to survive them.

But Barber's wayward lifestyle was steadily taking its toll

and, by 1851, suffering from rheumatic fever and also from gonorrhoea, he was a virtual invalid.

Ironically this brought the happiest and most peaceful period that the couple had ever enjoyed. Sarah became a caring and sympathetic wife, Joseph an extremely grateful husband. Dr Scott Smith and his assistant Thomas Mather made regular visits to the Barber home, and were deeply impressed by the care that Sarah was extending. But Barber's condition continued to deteriorate and soon it was clear that Sarah would no longer be able to cope on her own. She called upon a young shoemaker, Robert Ingram, who moved into their home and assisted Sarah in her nursing duties.

At length, however, Joseph Barber saw that the end was coming and felt it was time to settle his affairs. On March 11th, 1851, he made his will. He left the house and his three acres of land to Sarah. The land was too heavily mortgaged to be saleable, but it would, nevertheless, provide his wife with a steady income of 12 shillings a week. It was no mean sum in those days.

After Barber's will was executed his condition began to fluctuate rather strangely. On the following Sunday he appeared well and went with Ingram to Leavers public house in Bulwell. On the Tuesday he went out for a walk in the rain. But then, on the Wednesday, he became so ill that Sarah summoned his mother, who stayed the night.

When the morning came, Barber appeared to be so much improved that his mother went home. But during the afternoon. he suffered a relapse and by the evening a handful of friends had come to sit around what they now regarded as his death bed.

Joseph Barber's death should have passed without comment. It was, after all, long expected. But malicious tongues soon began to wag. A rumour, started up by Sarah's former lover, Gillott, suggested that all was not as it seemed. Barber had in fact been poisoned.

There was no substance to his claim, save for the fact that Sarah had occasionally threatened her husband's life.

But, once the rumour began, it had to be dealt with. A post-mortem was ordered.

The post-mortem procedure would have horrified a modern pathologist. One of the surgeons, for instance, walked home with Joseph's liver in his pocket. But, all the same, they found what it was they were looking for - arsenic, more than enough to kill a man.

Only two people, Sarah and Richard Ingram, had the opportunity to administer any poison to Joseph Barber. It was therefore assumed that one of them, or both, had to be guilty. They were therefore arrested and brought to trial.

Sarah Barber and Robert Ingram sat in the dock of Nottingham's Assizes. They were soberly dressed; Ingram in a black suit and Sarah in her widow's weeds. Ingram looked taught and nervous, while Sarah appeared almost lighthearted at times.

The prosecution made much of the threats uttered by Sarah, the income that she would inherit and the fact that no one else could have given Joseph the poison. The defence pointed out that the entire case was based on circumstantial evidence, and appealed to the jury's common sense by asking whether anyone contemplating murder would have acted so openly.

The trial ended on the second day with a decision split right down the middle. They found Sarah Barber guilty of wilful murder but Robert Ingram entirely innocent. On hearing this news, Ingram fell to his knee, and remained in this position while the judge, donning the black cap, passed the sentence of death upon Sarah.

Sarah accepted the verdict with remarkable composure. Turning towards the jury she said firmly: "Gentleman of the jury, if you have found me guilty in this world, you cannot prove me guilty in the next. Gentleman, I am not guilty. I am as innocent as a child just born."

The judge then signalled to her that she must now leave the dock. But, instead of doing so, Sarah turned and, seizing Ingram, lifted him bodily from his knees and kissed him passionately on the lips. The jailer, sensing that this could be the last embrace the two would ever share, waited a long moment before separating them.

But the story of Sarah Barber was far from over. Whilst she was in Nottingham jail, awaiting her execution, she asked to see Mr Hillyward, the prison governor. In his presence and that of a magistrate, she made the following statement:

"On the Sunday prior to my husband's death, Ingram bought some poison and mixed this with the medicine. I then administered this medicine unaware that it contained poison, and thus inadvertently killed my husband. Ingram didn't tell me what he'd done until after my husband's death."

Neither the governor nor the magistrate were over-impressed by her statement. The condemned frequently become inventive. Nevertheless, the governor was a humane man and had no wish to see Sarah hanged. Two days later he revisited her cell and said: "Sarah Barber, have you told the whole truth; is there anything else you can say? Your statement is not believed. Is there any way you can prove it?"

"Of course I can," she replied. "The medicine bottle which was used to poison my husband is in the outhouse; and if you talk to Robert Ingram he'll tell you the truth because he's an honest man."

They duly found the bottle containing medicine laced with arsenic. And when they questioned Ingram, he confirmed Sarah's story word for word. It placed him in a novel situation. He had been tried for murder and found not guilty. And now he was confessing. But his statement made it clear that Sarah was no murderess.

On August 13th, the Home Office issued a reprieve.

Robert Ingram was subsequently charged with felony and sentenced to jail. But, because he was regarded as a confused young man, he served a mercifully short sentence.

Sarah Barber was transported to Australia for life, arriving in the new continent just as their summer had begun.

The ill-luck that had dogged her life had now come to an end. She soon obtained a "ticket-of-leave," married a good, caring man and, it is said, lived happily ever after.

41

THE RED BARN MURDER

Maria Marten was a popular lass in the village of Polstead, Suffolk. An attractive girl, she had the pick of all the men from thereabouts. If accounts are to be believed, she picked the majority. Maria lost her virginity to one gentleman, had a child with a second and a miscarriage with a third. Lord knows how many other men there were in between. But, without a doubt, by the time she had settled on the hapless William Corder, in the spring of 1827, she was already a woman of the world.

Young William had hoped that he too would be one of Maria's easy dalliances. But he turned up too late. Having reached the ripe old age of 24, her father, the local mole catcher, had decided that now was the time his daughter should settle down. Frivolous affairs were henceforth, or at least temporarily, a thing of the past. Thus, when William Corder began spending his evenings making love to sweet Maria in the red barn on his father's farm, he was not engaged in the easy passion that he had assumed. He was setting himself up for wedlock.

There was much talk of the liberties he had already taken in Mr Marten's later discussion with young William. A wedding, the mole catcher declared, would have to be arranged.

William was less than enthusiastic about the idea but, being a rather weak-willed individual, he reluctantly agreed.

Prior to any preparations, however, he spoke to his newly announced fiancée and told her that a secret wedding, an elopement even, would be a far better solution to their problems.

Maria readily accepted William's plan, especially after he had told her that she might be arrested for having bastard children if they did it a different way. She arranged to meet him at the red barn on May 18th. William told her to dress in a suit of men's clothes, "the better," he said, "to ensure secrecy." They would then travel up to Ipswich in the horse and gig that would be waiting for them.

The appointment was kept, but there was no horse or gig in sight. Instead, as Maria's brother would later recall, William was waiting for her with a pickaxe. Maria Marten was never seen again.

Perhaps suprisingly, no questions were asked about her disappearance for quite a while. Indeed, it wasn't until two weeks later that Mrs Marten enquired of William where her daughter might be. William told her that she had been in Ipswich, sorting out the marriage papers, and would shortly be moving to the Isle of Wight, where he would join her. It was there, he said, that the two of them planned to live. This answer seemed to satisfy her and no more was said. Shortly afterwards, William bid Mr and Mrs Martin adieu and went off to meet his wife.

He travelled first to Ipswich and then to London, from where he wrote the Martens a number of letters, reassuring them that he and their daughter were enjoying married life immensely and were cheerfully content in their new Isle of Wight home. He also got married in reality, to a woman by the name of Mary Moore, the owner of a girls' school in Ealing.

All seemed well for a while, until Mrs Martin began to have nightmares. She dreamed that he daughter had been murdered and buried in the Corder's barn. The dream recurred night after night until, finally, she demanded that something was done.

Her husband went to the red barn and began digging

into the soil, applying himself most energetically to the spot that featured in his wife's dream. After a little while he came across a shawl, which he knew to be his daughter's. He dug down another foot or so, and came across a part of a human body. In the end, he unearthed the entire corpse of his murdered daughter.

An inquest was held where it was established that the body was, beyond doubt, that of Maria Marten, and that her death had been brought about by violence. Even though the body was in an in advanced state of decomposition, blood was clearly discernible on the face, neck and hair. There were stab wounds in her neck, on her face and in the orbit of the right eye. She had also been shot. But it seemed clear that the actual cause of death had been strangulation.

No one doubted for one moment that William Corder had to be the murderer. A search was made for him and he was eventually found, working as a headmaster, in Mary Moore's school.

At his trial, held at the Shire Hall, Bury St Edmunds, on August 7th, 1828, William Corder claimed innocence and said that Maria had killed herself. He explained that he and Maria had quarrelled and she had got into a terrible temper. He complained to her that, if this was going to be what married life was like, he wanted none of it and began to walk out of the barn. All of a sudden, he had heard the retort of a pistol. He spun around and there, before him, he saw his fiancée falling to the ground.

Corder admitted that he was very foolish to have tried to conceal the body and regretted he had done it. But, he said, he panicked.

It was an entertaining story, but one that nobody paid the least attention to. William Corder was convicted of murder and sentenced to death.

Back in the jail, and awaiting execution, the prison governor pleaded with him to confess. Finally, Corder blurted out "I am a guilty man. I am justly sentenced and may God forgive me."

William Corder was publicly hanged at Bury St Edmunds. He attracted a huge crowd of onlookers, even though the weather was appalling. As a grisly finishing touch, a strip of Corder's skin was later used to bind the official account of the case.

A book and a play were subsequently written about the murder and were both hugely successful. The story remains popular even today.

Maria Marten lies buried in the churchyard at Polstead Green, with just a little wooden plaque to mark the spot. The gravestone was chipped away long ago by souvenir hunters.

42

THE AXE WOMAN OF SURREY

For a woman convicted of only one slaying, the universal dislike and revulsion attached to the name of Kate Webster is truly awesome. And, indeed, so it should be. What other murderer would boil their dismembered victim, skim off the fat and try to sell it in their local pub as "best dripping"? Webster's killings may have been short on number, but they were long on gore.

Kate Webster was born in Killann, County Wexford, Ireland, in 1849 and, even as a child, she was a horror. Her parents, respectable but poor people, found her virtually unmanageable. In the end, even the local priest, who was called many times to the Webster household to lecture the young girl, gave up on her. When, in her early teens, Kate announced she was leaving home for Liverpool everyone breathed a sigh of relief.

For several years Kate lived by stealing, with the consequence that, at 18, she was sentenced to four years' imprisonment. When she was released she went to London and resumed her old ways until the birth of her son, which temporarily slowed her down.

To pick up extra money, Kate lived as a boarding-house robber, which entailed moving into rooms, then selling the furniture and fittings before moving on. At this she was fairly inept, for she was jailed several times.

In January 1879, 30-year-old Kate and her son lived off

the charity of a Mrs Crease, who was able to find her work in the domestic service of a wealthy widow, Mrs Martha Julia Thomas, who lived at 2 Vine Cottages, Park Road, Richmond. For the first time in her life, it seemed as though Kate had turned over a new leaf. She took to her duties seriously and with every appearance of being anxious to give satisfaction. Mrs Thomas was delighted. "I think she will turn out to be a real treasure," the woman confided to a friend.

Unfortunately this happy state of domestic bliss between mistress and servant did not continue for long. Within a month Kate had reverted to her old ways, neglecting her work and spending most of her day drinking at a pub called the Hole in the Wall. This was particularly annoying to Mrs Thomas, who was not on speaking terms with the landlady there.

Soon enough the day came when Mrs Thomas, tight-lipped and close to anger, spoke to her servant about her changed ways. The old woman was amazed by the girl's response. Kate screamed at her and rained down a storm of protest on her employer. Mrs Thomas, not wishing to provoke her further, retired.

The situation did not improve and Mrs Thomas never got any happier. Kate continued to ignore her work and, furthermore, things started to disappear from the house. Several trinkets vanished, as well as garments the widow had stowed in a chest-of-drawers. By now the old lady knew that if she made any criticism of her servant she would merely find herself on the receiving end of a torrent of abuse. It would be a pointless exercise. No, she reasoned, enough is enough. Kate Webster would have to go.

On Sunday, March 2nd, 1879, a nervous Mrs Thomas gave Kate notice. As expected, the girl screeched curses at her, but Mrs Thomas paid no heed. Instead she went quietly off to church to attend the afternoon service. She returned home later, happy to find that the house was empty. She went to her bedroom and lay down.

Just as Mrs Thomas was nodding off, the door to her

bedroom swung open and Kate Webster, eyes full of rage, burst in. She was clutching an axe.

The old woman stared in horror as the weapon crashed down on her. She staggered under the blow but managed to right herself before she hit the floor. Summoning all the strength at her command, she pushed Kate through the open door of the bedroom and on to the landing. There the two women grappled, swaying and panting, each trying to force the other to her knees. Martha Thomas, however, was no match for her assailant. She lost her balance and toppled backwards. Kate leaped towards her and, seizing her torso in a brutal grip, pitched the old woman down the stairs.

Mrs Thomas was injured by the fall and many of her bones had been broken. But she was not yet dead. Pitifully, she looked up at her servant, pleading for mercy. Kate stood over her scornfully, paying no attention to the cries. Wielding the axe high in the air, she slammed it down into the old woman's body. Martha Thomas had breathed her last.

But Kate had not yet finished. Now she dragged the body into the small scullery and, by the light of a flickering candle, stripped it naked. Then, with knife and axe, she began to cut. With horrendous brutality she sliced at the flesh and sawed at the bones. She prised open the corpse's mouth and yanked out her gold mouth-plate. She ripped at the limbs, broke off the fingers then, like she had once cut firewood, she hacked and chopped and cut until the old woman's body was nothing but a series of lumps of meat.

Moving to the hearth, Kate lit the fire and watched the flames lap up around the large copper cauldron. She filled the cauldron with water and waited for it to boil. Then, when it was good and steamy, she picked up the butchered pieces of flesh and threw them into the pot.

The sickening stew boiled for hours. So repugnant was the smell that even Kate found herself wanting to retch and she left the kitchen for the clean air of outside. But, in an hour or so she was back, watching the disgusting casserole simmer and steam. The sickly liquid changed colour, getting darker and darker. It also became thicker, more glutinous. Now Kate was satisfied that the boiling water had done all that it could do and the fire was allowed to die down. Some time later, in that reeking, putrid atmosphere, Kate Webster began the gruesome work of packaging the part-boiled remains of her employer. Some smashed bones and bleached chunks of flesh were crammed into a large box. More were wrapped in a capacious leather bag, more still were parcelled with sheets of paper. Legend has it that Webster skimmed the fat from the surface of the straw, placing the contents in two jars. When these had set, she would sell them as "dripping."

How Kate slept that night will never be known. But, in the evening she was in the tavern and appeared in high spirits. She had lost no time in selling her mistress's gold-mouth plate and was cheerfully spending that money on ale.

Kate woke up the following day feeling better than she had done for months. She had a tremendous sense of energy and an urge to take up the threads from old times. Her mind turned backwards to forgotten friends and past acquaintances. In particularly, to the Porter family who lived in Hammersmith on the other side of the Thames. Equipped with seven or eight pounds of the murdered woman's money in her purse, the widow's elegant clothes on her back and a large leather bag in her hand, she set off to pay them a visit.

The Porters greeted her warmly. In her stolen finery, Kate Webster appeared elegant and refined and, soon enough, she was gathered in the living room with all the family, supping some tea and making conversation.

Webster confided to the Porters how a dear aunt had died quite recently and left her a small house in Richmond.

"It's a very nice place," she told them, "but I'm anxious to dispose of the furniture."

She looked inquiringly round the tea-table. Henry Porter glanced at his son: "How about John Church, Bob?"

"He might take it" Robert Porter agreed cautiously.

For three hours or more, Kate continued drinking tea

and spinning tales to keep her listeners' eyes wide. Then, as quickly as she had come, she rose and said she must be going. Kate picked up her leather bag and made her way to the door.

Robert Porter said he would accompany her to the station and his offer was gratefully accepted. He took the bag from her hand and led the way.

As it turned out Robert and Kate did not go directly to the train. Instead they lingered in a number of local taverns. At one Kate excused herself, saying she had to meet a friend who was waiting for her in Barnes. She wouldn't be long, she said, begged Robert to wait for her.

Kate returned some 20 minutes later.

"Where's your bag?" asked Robert.

"I left it with my friend," she told him.

Robert then decided to accompany Kate to her home. When they arrived, she asked him for a favour. She had a large box she needed to carry to Richmond Bridge, could he help her? "I'd be obliged, Bob," she said, "if you would help me with it to the middle of the bridge, then leave me."

It was an odd request but Robert agreed and he manfully carried the wooden chest to the centre of the bridge and set it down. Then he walked back the way he had come.

He hadn't gone very far when he heard a loud splash. A couple of minutes later running footsteps sounded behind him. He turned as Kate Webster caught up with him, She was smiling and her plain face was animated. "There!" she exclaimed. "It's over."

The next day fishermen found the grisly contents of the box: the cooked remains of a human being.

This gruesome find, however, was not connected to the disappearance of Julia Thomas until some time later. That happened when, true to their word, the Porters had put Kate in contact with John Church and he had arranged to buy all Mrs Thomas's old furniture. For this he paid Kate the grand sum of £68.

As Church's van pulled up outside Mrs Thomas's home and the furniture was beginning to be removed, Mrs

Thomas's next door neighbour became suspicious. She supposed that Mr Church must be a thief.

The furniture man was arrested and taken in for questioning. It was then that the whole gruesome tale began to come together.

Kate fled, back to Killann in Ireland, but was arrested 10 days later, wearing her victim's fine clothes and jewellery.

Right up to the night of her execution Kate proclaimed her innocence and wildly accused anyone she could think of as being the real murderer. Finally, however, on the day of her execution, she admitted her guilt to the prison chaplain.

Kate Webster was hanged at Wandsworth Prison on July 29th, 1879. Before dying she cursed the hangman in the most appalling language.

43

MRS DYER, THE BABY FARMER

A doctor called by the police confirmed the cause of death was strangulation. But there was also something else. Written on the inside of the brown paper was a name and a Reading, Berkshire, address, still legible despite long immersion. The paper had once wrapped a parcel sent to the home of Mrs Amelia Dyer. Not that she was there any more. A frequent mover, she was now at another address in Caversham. And, by the time the police caught up with her, two more babies were found in the river.

From the moment that the police knocked on her front door, the carefully cultivated reputation of Mrs Amelia Dyer, sometime member of the Salvation Army, began to crumble. Not only was she Mrs Dyer, she had also been known as Mrs Thomas, Mrs Harding and Mrs Stanfield. Her home contained no end of baby clothes, but few babies. More baby clothes were found at the Willesden home of her married daughter. But, again, there were no infants to wear them.

Who could have entrusted the care of their offspring to this gruesome woman? What thoughtless mother could have left her children in Mrs Dyer's charge?

One was Evelina Edith Marmon, a Cheltenham barmaid. At a time when the plight of unmarried mothers was much worse than it is today, Evelina had given birth to an illegitimate daughter, Doris. With no money to keep the child, she scanned the columns of the newspapers for offers of adoption. One of them, more attractively worded than the rest, caught her eye; she sat down to answer it. In a day or so, she received a reply:

> Dear Madam,
> In reference to your letter of adoption of a child, I beg to say that I shall be glad to have a dear little baby girl, one that I can bring up and call my own.
> First I must tell you that we are plain, homely people in fairly good circumstances. I have a good and comfortable home. I am alone a great deal, and I don't want a child for money's sake, but for company and comfort. A child with me will have a good home, and a mother's love and care. We belong to the Church of England. I hope to hear from you again.
> Yours faithfully,
> Annie Amelia Stanfield P.S. What a sweet name Doris is I am sure she is a sweet little soul.

The writer seemed to be a kind, motherly person: just the sort Evelina was after, provided she didn't ask or more than the girl could pay.

Relieved to find that Mrs Stanfield would take Doris for £10, Evelina decided that somehow or other she would raise the money. She wrote accepting the offer, only asking that she might sometimes be allowed to come down and visit her baby.

"I shall be only too pleased for you to come and see me sometimes," answered Mrs Stanfield. "I assure you that it would be as great a treat to us as the chance would be to you. I should really feel more comfortable to know the dear little soul had someone who really cared for her. I shall value her all the more, rest assured."

Amelia added that her husband (from whom, in reality, she had been long separated) idolized children. She also told Miss Marmon that they had a lovely orchard at the back of their house where she was sure Doris would love to play and get some fresh air.

A short while later Amelia Dyer travelled to the Midlands and met the young mother and her child.

Evelina found the woman larger than she had expected – she weighed over fifteen stone – and also, at 57, somewhat older. Moreover, with her grim face and a tightly screwed knob of grey hair protruding from her, she looked very different to the kindly woman that Evelina had imagined. But she gushed over little Doris and seemed to be genuinely besotted by her. As she pronounced her to be a little love, and tenderly wrapped her in the shawl she had thoughtfully brought with her, Evelina was won over. Giving her baby a tearful kiss she waved goodbye and watched Mrs Stanfield depart, carrying Doris in her arms.

Less than a month later, Reading residents were shocked by the discovery of first one, then six more babies, dragged from the depths of the Thames. Doris, found sharing a carpet bag with a baby boy, was one of them.

Each child had been strangled with a bootlace or a length of tape, and each had been weighted with a brick.

It was little Harry Simmons who finally gave the game away. It was his carpet bag, he said, that had been brought up from the bottom of the Thames. The nine-year-old orphan had arrived with it when he was put in the care of Mrs Dyer about a year ago. He said that, since Christmas, there had been about 25 children in the Dyer home, ranging in age from a few weeks to ten years. He didn't know where those children were now.

When she pleaded guilty at the Old Bailey on May 22nd, 1896, the only defence that she could offer was that she was insane. That plea was rejected and, in her sombre black dress and cap, she listened with downcast eyes and twitching lips as the horrific evidence built up against her.

The jury was absent for only six minutes before deciding on her guilt. When they returned Dyer was in a state of complete collapse, and two warders and wardresses had to lift her from her chair as the verdict of guilty was read out and the sentence of death was passed.

The Judge told her. "You slew these children for sordid gain, and in order that your guilt might be concealed, you buried these poor little ones beneath the water of the Thames. I wish I could suppose that your guilt and wickedness stopped here. I am sadly afraid, however, from all that I have heard, that you must have carried on this cruel and wicked business for many a long day... Pray in the meantime, until your end comes, to Him who alone can pardon your great sin, to be more merciful to you than you were to these poor, innocent, unprotected infants."

Prior to her execution, Amelia Dyer made a feeble attempt to strangle herself by twisting a handkerchief round her throat. She was subsequently under the constant supervision of eight wardresses.

She was hanged at Newgate on June 10th, 1896.

Just how many children met their death at the hands of Amelia Dyer, nobody will ever know. Although the corpses of seven of her victims were found, in the six months prior to her arrest more than 40 strangled babies had been recovered from the Thames. She told one of her warders. "you'll know mine by the tape around their necks."

44

THE MONSTROUS METYARDS

Sarah Metyard, who was ostensibly a milliner, lived with her daughter, also called Sarah, in the East End of London during the middle part of the eighteenth century. There was no man in their house but both women had passionate love affairs.

They were an attractive couple. The daughter was very beautiful and although the looks of her mother had suffered the ravages of time, she too, for her age, was a shapely, comely woman.

Their pleasing outward appearance, however, concealed as dark a pair of hearts as there has ever been. They were vicious, sadistic, brutal, gruesome and callous. Who knows how many fell victim to their hand?

The first indication that all was not as it should be came soon after these women, under cover of darkness, crept from their home carrying a large basket of parcels. They did not go far. A stream flowed past the end of the alley where they lived and here the load was deposited.

Their disposal method on this occasion, however, did not prove very efficient. That very night a watchman on his rounds noticed that a sewer grating was blocked. He gave the parcels a tentative poke with a rod. They seemed ominously soft, and he pulled them out. Peeling off the wrappings he was horrified to find that they contained human remains.

He reported his gruesome find at once to the authorities and all the parcels were recovered, opened and examined. When pieced together, they were found to form the corpse of a girl.

There was no means of identifying the dismembered young female and, consequently, at the inquest, the coroner declared that there was only one possible solution to the mystery. The remains must be those of a body stolen from a grave which had, for some reason, been discarded. His view carried weight, for it was then a common enough practice for certain criminals to rob graves and sell the bodies to surgeons. Thus, this first-to-be-found victim of the Metyards was, in time, forgotten.

Some four years later, a handsome young man called Charles Rooker came seeking lodgings at the house where the two Sarahs lived. Never missing an opportunity to make extra money, they took in the young man and he stayed for six months.

Both women lost no time in finding opportunities to display themselves to him and to make it clear that their beds were available whenever he wanted. So it came as no surprise when, one night, he was openly approached by both mother and daughter with an unusual proposition. If he would take them both as wives - or at least sexually regard them and treat them as such - then he would not be expected to pay any more rent for his rooms.

Rooker, who in common with many young men of his age and station, was always short of cash and ever eager for sex, readily agreed to this bizarre arrangement and, for some time, he made love alternately to mother and daughter.

Slowly, however, it began to dawn on him that all was not well in the house. To begin with he had supposed that the elder Sarah was nothing more sinister than what she purported to be, a milliner who accepted young girls as apprentices. But then it struck him as strange that these girls, without exception, came from families who, for one reason or another, were anxious to be rid of them. And then he began to notice her treatment of them.

Sarah's abuse of the girls was horrifically sadistic. She beat her apprentices often, sometimes even resorting to the extreme of stripping the girls naked and tying them up hand and foot, starving them of food and drink for long periods and thrashing them unmercifully whenever she felt like it. Rooker discovered that it was not unusual for Sarah to beat her girls unconscious, and beyond.

Eventually it became too much for him to live with, so Charles Rooker did the only thing possible. He decided to move out.

By now, however, his attachment to the daughter had grown strong and he informed her of his plans to leave. He asked if she would join him and live as his mistress in another house along the street.

The idea appealed to Sarah, who had recently had a bitter argument with her mother and wanted to teach her a lesson. She readily agreed to Charles Rooker's suggestion and taunted the older woman with her news.

Sarah's mother flew into a rage when she heard their plans. She ranted and raved at the couple, cajoled them and threatened them. Finally she resorted to tearfully begging her daughter "not to leave her alone and destitute." The young Sarah, however, was immune to her mother's pleadings.

Now the old woman tried bribery. She offered Rooker her jewellery, which she swore was worth at least a thousand guineas, if he would switch his affections, drop Sarah and live with her. To Rooker, who had no money, this was a strong temptation, one that he would find hard to resist. When young Sarah saw him hesitate, she acted in desperation.

"If he stays with you," she shrieked at her mother, "then I'll go to the police and tell them who it was in those Chick Lane parcels! I'll tell the police all about Annie Naylor. I'll tell them everything."

Her mother blanched, shattered by the threat. Without further argument, she left the couple to their plans. But

Charles Rooker had now heard more than was good for his peace of mind. He questioned Sarah continually, until she told him everything.

She recounted how Annie Naylor had been thrashed so savagely that she had died. She told him how her mother had cut up the girl's body, parcelled up the pieces, and dumped them into the Chick Lane sewer. Young Sarah confessed that at least two other girls had died as a result of fearful beatings from her mother. Their bodies, too, had been dismembered and disposed of in a similar manner.

Charles Rooker was horrified by the stories and, although he was aware that the young Sarah might also be arrested, he ignored her pleas to keep quiet and did what he felt was the right thing to do. He told everything he had heard to the police.

After the two Sarahs were jointly charged, more of their chilling story came out. For years they had indulged in horrific behaviour. Young girls in their charge had been subjected to brutal beatings, physical outrages and unspeakable atrocities. Many deaths had occurred at their hands. The exact number of victims was unknown.

At the trial, old Sarah tried to place the entire blame for the beatings, abuses and murders on her daughter. Young Sarah denied everything. It was her mother, she insisted, who committed the crimes.

Both were found equally guilty and sentenced to death.

Shortly before the sentences were carried out, young Sarah made a free confession. She revealed how, coerced by her mother, she had helped her to kill the girls, cut them up and dispose of their bodies.

On the morning of the women's execution, July 19th, 1768, old Sarah Metyard had to be carried by force from her cell and put into the hangman's cart. Her daughter showed a different mettle, climbing with some dignity, unaided, into the cart.

When they reached the gibbet, old Sarah fainted and had to be forcibly revived so that she would be conscious when the hangman's rope was placed around her neck. Young Sarah showed no emotion at all.

45

THE HARRIDAN OF HAMPSTEAD

Styllou Christofi was the mother-in-law from hell. A rough, ill educated peasant woman from Cyprus, she had already shown her mettle when, at the age of 24, she killed her own mother-in-law by jamming a burning stick down her throat. Thirty years later, when she was a mother-in-law herself, she behaved no better.

Christofi had five children but it was Stavros for whom she reserved her special attention. He was, after all, her only son. When, in 1937, he left his small village to seek his fortune in England, she was intensely proud. But she was also insanely jealous. Why couldn't she be with him too? And what was wrong with her home that her son should want to leave it?

Yet, if she felt bad in 1937, she felt worse five years later. It was then that her son married Hella, not the nice Greek girl she had recommended, but a striking, independent and intelligent German woman, a true daughter of the Ruhr.

All this mattered little to Stavros, however. He was enjoying his time in London and achieving considerable success. Soon he and Hella had three delightful children and he himself held a respected post as wine waiter at the Café de Paris in the West End. They had found themselves a comfortable home in South Hill Park, Hampstead and Hella had proved herself to be a good mother and an excellent housewife. Memories of his mother had receded.

His old village in the Cyprus mountains, almost forgotten.

In 1953, however, Stavros's new life of contentment came to a very abrupt end. His mother came over to visit, ostensibly just long enough to earn the money to buy some land in Cyprus. A year later, however, she was still there and she was still driving the couple mad.

Stavros and Hella had both anticipated the difficulties of her arrival. An ignorant peasant woman set down in London, unable to speak a word of English, confronting a daughter-in-law and three grandchildren for the first time in her life, was bound to have problems. They were as sympathetic to her as they could manage. But, from the start she had been utterly impossible.

She hated the house and, with the single exception of her son, everybody in it. She was particularly scathing about Hella, and the way she spent money. And she also didn't like her make-up, her dress sense, the way she brought up her children, the way she looked, the way she spoke and the way she breathed. There was nothing that Hella could do that could please her. Eventually it all got too much. To avert a looming disaster Stavros arranged for his wife to take their children for a holiday at her parents' home in Germany.

Upon Hella's return, it was decided that Stavros's 53-year-old mother would have to go back to Cyprus. Stavros and Hella told her as tactfully as they could.

"If you feel like that about it, I shall go," said Mrs Christofi. She had got the message.

Happy for the first time in weeks, Stavros kissed his wife goodbye as he left for work on the evening of July 28th. At last, he thought, the problem has been solved. Little did he know what lay in store.

The children were safely tucked up in their beds and Hella was preparing for a bath, when Styllou Christofi struck. Picking up the cast iron ashplate from the stove, she brought it crashing down on to Hella's skull. Snatching one of the children's scarves, she wound it around the unconscious woman's throat, turning it and twisting it until it began to cut into her neck. Then, dragging the corpse into the back garden, she soaked the body in kerosene and lit it with a match. As the flames began to rise, she noticed the wedding ring on Hella's finger. Grabbing hold of it, she yanked it off and put it into her own pocket. Then she watched her daughter-in-law burn.

A neighbour, John Young, saw the blaze, but must have assumed that it was merely a garden fire. No doubt he was reassured when he saw Mrs Christofi come out from the flat and appear to stoke it up. But as the evening drew on, the fire grew out of control and even Mrs Christofi got worried.

Just before one o'clock a London restaurateur, Mr Burstoff, was returning home with his wife. As he drove slowly past Hampstead railway station Mrs Christofi ran up to their car.

"Please come! Fire burning! Children sleeping!" she cried.

The Burstoffs went with her to the flat, but could see no sign of a fire. Where was the blaze, asked Mr Burstoff.

"Shush! Babies sleeping!" said Mrs Christofi. Then she opened the French windows.

"Look!" cried Mrs Burstoff. "There's somebody on the ground."

Mr Burstoff saw the head of a nearly naked body covered in blood. He told Mrs Christofi he had to phone the police and dashed inside.

As they were waiting for the police to arrive, Mrs Christofi began her garbled explanation:

"Me smell burning. Me come down. Me pour water, but she died."

Once in police custody, Styllou Christofi offered a fuller explanation.

"When I went to bed Hella and I were on perfectly good terms and she said that she was going to do some washing, I do not know whether she meant clothes or whether she was going to wash herself. Every evening Hella washes the whole of her body with water."

Mrs Christofi went on to say that at about 12.55 p.m. she

got up and saw smoke. Hella was lying in the garden. "I saw little flames at the ankles, around the knees, on both arms and the back of the head. I put some water in a bowl and splashed it over her with my hand. I called her by name, and touched her face and hand, and then I got some more water and threw it over her."

This account, however, did not square with the evidence given by her neighbour, who had seen her in the garden at 11.30. Nor did it square with any of the forensic evidence or the results of the post-mortem. Eventually the true story emerged. Styllou Christofi was arrested.

Mrs Christofi's legal counsel urged her to plead insanity, but this advice was angrily rejected. In court, with little English, but accompanied by an interpreter, she had not much to say. After the verdict and the sentence of death, she asked to speak, but her request was ignored.

Whilst awaiting execution she expressed great disappointment in Stavros. She had come to England, she said, because she could no longer bear to be apart from him. But he had tried too hard to hang her, "to put around my neck the noose, so that you may rest." She refused to see him when he called at the jail. She was still angry with him when she met her end.

Styllou Christofi was hanged at Holloway Prison on December 13th, 1954, the first woman to be hanged in London in more than thirty years.

46

THE FRUSTRATED SPINSTER POISONINGS

Few people paid much heed to the tragic death of little Sidney Barker, though it was a mystery how the poison had got into the four-year old's bag of chocolates. But Miss Christiana Edmunds would not keep quiet. At the boy's inquest she demanded to have her say, and have her say she did.

The 42-year-old spinster stood up and declared that she too had brought chocolate creams at Mr Maynard's which had made her very ill. "I bought some in September last," she said. "I ate two and felt sick and I gave some to a friend, who was also ill. I had violent internal pains and a burning in my throat. I took some brandy, which made me worse, and then some castor oil." Miss Edmunds then went on to say that, in March, she had again bought some sweets from the shop. "I ate a portion of a white one," she declared, "but the taste was so bad I could not eat any more. It tasted like copper. I was ill about ten minutes after."

Miss Edmunds's evidence continued for some time and concluded with her account of an unsatisfactory meeting she had with Mr and Mrs Maynard and her consequent action of having the chocolates analysed. It appeared that her chocolates, too, contained strychnine.

After Miss Edmunds had said her piece, Mr Maynard was naturally called to account. All he was able to say, however, was that he could not understand how any poison could get into his chocolates. His children ate them regularly and had never been ill. Mr George Robert Ware, who actually manufactured the chocolates, was the next to be summoned. He, too, was perplexed by the episode. He could not see how it could have happened. But he did admit that he sometimes used poison to kill rats.

This was the information the jury had been waiting to hear. It was all that was needed to settle their minds. When the time came they declared their verdict promptly and with ease.

"We find that the child died from poisoning by strychnine," they announced, "but we quite exonerate Mr Maynard from blame, and the other gentleman also, though we think he might be a little more careful in killing the rats."

The inquest was now over, everyone could return to their homes.

But Christiana Edmunds was not content. She was outraged that the inquest failed to attach blame to anyone. A week letter she sent a letter to the dead boy's father to point out this injustice. She said the same in another letter the next day, and in a third the following week. She didn't sign them herself, however, but dispatched them anonymously as if they had been written by three different people.

To anyone who knew her, it was clear that Christiana had a personal interest in this matter, and it wasn't merely because she had fallen ill with the chocolates herself. Mr Maynard's chocolates had done more than damage her health, they had damaged her pride.

It had happened at the home of Dr Beard, a man with whom, if the truth be told, Christiana was madly in love. She had gone to visit him at the end of October 1870, six months before little Sidney Barker had died, and happened to take a bag of Mr Maynard's chocolates with her. She had offered one to the doctor's haughty wife, and the lady had accepted. But the chocolates were of the poisoned kind, and foul in taste. Mrs Beard had spat it out. Even so she was a little ill afterwards.

Dr Beard had been upset by the incident. He even

mplied that Christiana had attempted murder. He made it clear the she was no longer welcome at 64, Grand Parade, Brighton, and invited her to leave. What little intimacy there had been between the spinster and the doctor came to an abrupt stop. Christiana was mortified.

Some time later, in August 1871, packets of cakes, preserved fruits and sweetmeats were being received by various people in Brighton. These packages were usually accompanied by notes saying they were for certain members of the family, and came from an old friend. Some of these notes bore the initials "G.M." others were signed more cryptically. The recipients of these parcels were glad enough when they arrived, but usually regretted it soon after. Generally they had been taken ill and had to call the doctor.

In due course one of these boxes arrived at Dr Beard's home, addressed to his wife. It contained cakes, preserved fruits and ginger bread-nuts. The note, wrapped around a plum cake about the size of a tea-cup, read as follows: "A few home-made cakes for the children. Those done up are flavoured on purpose for yourself to enjoy. You will guess who this is from; I can't mystify you, I fear. I hope this will arrive for you in time while the things are still fresh."

Mrs Beard cut the cake open the following Saturday and noticed something in it which looked like unbaked flour. She turned up her nose in disapproval and handed the cake to her servant to dispose of. The servants in the house, however, were not as fussy as their mistress and two of them tried the cake later that afternoon. Both were violently sick.

It was then that the police were called in. The box and the note were passed over. So too were Dr Beard's early suspicions about Christiana Edmunds.

Christiana was promptly arrested and charged with "attempting to administer poison to Mrs Beard." As time went by, however, the charges began to grow. A Mrs Boys and a Mr Garrett had also received presents of poisoned cakes and sweetmeats and suffered the consequence. Other cases too, started to be reported. And then, as the evidence piled up, Christiana Edmunds was also connected with the episode of Mr Maynard's poisoned chocolates. Soon she was facing a charge of murder, for the death of Sidney Barker.

The trial of Christiana Edmunds took place at the Old Bailey in January 1872.

As it progressed it became clear that Christiana was the culprit. It was found that she had made several purchases of strychnine from the local chemist. It was revealed that she left bags of poisoned chocolates lying around where others would pick them up. It was also shown that the anonymous letters sent to Sydney Barker's father, the note accompanying Mrs Beard's parcel of cakes and the notes that went with other similar parcels elsewhere, were all written in her hand.

Evidently Christiana had wanted to kill Mrs Beard and had thought that, if it appeared as though she was just one victim of a random campaign of poisoning, with other victims too, including herself, neither the police nor Beard, would ever suspect.

The jury found Christiana Edmunds guilty of murder and, though they were given the opportunity, they did not find her insane. She was therefore sentenced to death.

Ultimately, however, the death penalty was not inflicted. A claim of insanity was upheld.

47

THE PARISIAN BLUEBEARD

Even though he was balding and past fifty, women adored Henri Désiré Landru. His cheery laugh and amusing turn of phrase had them swooning at his feet. Charm and romance personified he was, in short, the personality boy among mass murderers.

In the early days of his career, Landru steered clear of killing, however. It wasn't that he didn't like violence, it was more that he felt it wasn't necessary. He had simply enticed his victims with the prospect of marriage, stripped them of their wealth and disappeared. When he set his sights on the attractive widow who had entered the Paris nightclub, however, he found himself having to contend with a complication. Mme Georges Cuchet had a son.

To begin with, the seduction followed his normal plan. As usual he introduced himself to the woman using a false identity. This time he was Raymond Daird, a wealthy engineer and a bachelor. He explained that he had never married because he had been devoted to his aged mother. Now that she was dead, he was looking for a wife. Mme Cuchet was flattered by his advances, and even more so by the flowers she began to receive and the other small gifts that were sent by her admirer. By the time Landru had offered to pay for her son's education. the widow was completely won over. Then the engagement ring arrived.

It was in the autumn of 1914 that Landru suggested to

Mme Cuchet that she should give him her life savings. This money, he informed her, would be invested on her behalf. He also told her she may as well sell her furniture. She wouldn't need it now, he explained, because he was taking her and her son André to a beautiful little villa he had rented in the village of Vernoillet. There, he declared, they would be able to marry and settle down.

Landru had always looked on seduction as a business, as a commercial way of earning a livelihood. He thus kept a diary that detailed all the expenses that his occupation incurred: flowers, meals, clothes, travel and so on. He also kept a record of the income that his exploits provided. That night, therefore, he entered the sum he had received for furnishings belonging to Mme Cuchet, and her rather meagre life savings. He then closed the book and made ready for the journey.

Landru had no intention of staying at Vernoillet for long and in a matter of weeks he was back on the train to Paris, eager to line up another poor woman to seduce and swindle. Foolishly, however, he had left behind a little valise containing some personal papers – very personal papers. André found this valise and opened it. He discovered that Monsieur Daird's real name was Landru, that he was married and the father of five children. What is more, he was preying on the affections of women other than André's mother.

It speaks well of Landru's charm that, when he returned to the villa that night and was confronted with the full facts of his disreputable life, he managed to explain everything away. He admitted he was married and that he had had other affairs. But all that, he said, was before he met Mme Cuchet. He loved her with a true and powerful passion. She alone was the one true love of his life. He had lied to her about himself only for fear of losing her. His wife he would divorce. The other women? He dismissed them with a wave of the hand as being of no consequence.

Within the hour, Mme Cuchet was back under his spell. André, however, was harder to convince. The boy, Landru knew, would remain a problem. He racked his brains to find a solution, but simply didn't know what to do. Then a smile appeared on his lips.

In January 1915, Landru was a very busy man, working in his garden behind the villa. He would dart in and out of the house at all hours, particularly at night; he seemed always to be in the process of starting, attending to or extinguishing a fire. His neighbours noticed the activity, of course, but none paid much attention to it. Four years later, however, they were to recall that, from the moment Landru became so involved with his gardening, Mme Cuchet and André were seen no more.

It was late in May, 1915, little more than a year after he had met Mme Cuchet, that Landru, now describing himself as a widower with two daughters, inserted an advertisement in a newspaper for a nurse for his girls. Mme Laborde-Line, a native of Argentina and the widow of a hotel proprietor, was one of the ladies who replied. A fairly attractive woman in her late forties, Mme Laborde-Line was, as Landru must have noticed, an individual of some means. Although her husband had left her well off, she had become a children's nurse to fend off her loneliness.

Landru had two young daughters and he produced them for Mme Laborde-Line when they met in a furnished room in Paris. What the children went back and told their mother is not recorded, but it has to be assumed that Mme Landru had long since grown used to hearing practically anything about her spouse. In any case, the children were not needed for long.

Mme Laborde-Line, positively wilted under Landru's charm and all talk of her prospective employment as a nurse soon evaporated. They had far more important things to discuss. She watched in delight as M. Cuchet (as Landru was now calling himself) become utterly besotted by her. He wrote her love letters, courted her around town and entertained her with what excitement wartime Paris still had to offer.

Talk of marriage was soon in the air. Landru declared he

would love to marry her there and then. Unfortunately, however, he had lost his identity papers. The actual ceremony would have to wait until he could obtain the necessary new credentials. In the meantime it was off to the villa in Vernouillet.

Mme Laborde-Line possessed a handsome blue dressing gown. Neighbours of Vernoillet saw her in the garden, picking summer flowers, wearing the gown. They saw her almost every day through the month of June. But then they didn't see her any more. They saw, instead, more of those fires. M. duPont, as he was known to them, was apparently a man who accumulated a great deal of garden rubbish.

In August the neighbours saw the blue dressing gown once again. This time, however, someone else was wearing it, a rather different creature to her predecessor, large, broad and ugly. M. duPont's taste in mistresses was evidently deteriorating. Still, they didn't have to tolerate her unattractive appearance for long. Later that month she too had disappeared from the Vernoillet landscape and the fires began again.

It was late in November 1915 when Landru journeyed to the small village of Gambais where, again under the name of M. duPont, he rented another home. This was a small, four-roomed stone residence behind a row of trees and half a mile from its nearest neighbour. Though rejoicing in the grand name of Villa Ermitage it was a run down place, damp, dark and forbidding. It had neither lights nor plumbing. But Landru seemed happy with it. His only cause for complaint was the stove. He wanted something larger, much larger. So he installed what amounted to a small furnace, a contraption so big that it required him to also install a tall, metal chimney that poked out of the villa's roof.

Landru's first guest at Gambais was one Mme Heon, a widow in her forties, whom he met through one of his advertisements in the newspaper. Mme Heon had just lost a son at the front and a daughter through illness. She was thus alone in the world and eager for Landru's embrace.

Little could she have known that, even before she had set foot on the train, that embrace was destined to be fatal.

Ever meticulous, Landru continued to keep a detailed written record of every one of his enterprises. One day early in December he had recorded, among other expenses in connection with Mme Heon, the cost of railway tickets for the journey from Paris. His ticket was a return, hers a single. The fires that had burned so vigorously in Vernoillet were now rekindled in Gambais. The heavy smoke bellowed for the new metal chimney.

Landru now became more active than he had ever been before in his life. Every fortnight or so he would bring a different woman up from Paris. Very rarely did they return. There were fires, fires and more fires. Even when the weather was warm the burning would continue. Indeed, even the middle of summer, when the dogs of Gambais lay panting in the shade, Landru would be piling up sacks of coal to keep his furnace glowing.

The fires continued to burn for more than three years. Landru must have felt immune from capture. On a sunny Saturday morning in April 1919, however, the Bluebeard's luck finally ran out.

Landru was strolling along the Rue de Rivoli when he came face to face with a lady who looked as if she recognized him from somewhere. This was not so unusual, of course. Having seduced, robbed and cheated hundreds of women in his time, a chance encounter with one of them was almost inevitable. He had developed a technique for dealing with such situations; he just pretended not to notice. He made a detour into a shop that sold china, hoping that the woman would move on.

As he selected an item, paid for his purchase and left his card, Landru was oblivious to the fact that the woman was still gazing at him. In taking his leave, he tipped his hat to the cashier. That did it. When she saw his white, shiny head, his observer recognized him as the man who, two years before, had promised marriage to her sister and escorted her to who knows where.

The woman, a Mlle Lacoste, went immediately to the Sureté. There she informed Inspector Bellin that her sister, Mme Guillen, had gone away with one M. Fremyet and she had not heard from her since. She told the inspector she had just seen the man in a china shop.

Inspector Bellin went to the shop and learned that the bald-headed customer was Lucien Guillet, of 76 Rue de Rochechouart. He then went straight to that address and arrested the man. Such an easy arrest after all Lanru's misdemeanours seems hardly credible.

Bellin retrieved Landru's diary and the police slowly began to build up a case. The gruesome book contained more than three hundred names, and the police addressed themselves to the unglamourous but vital chore of tracking down all the women in the book. Many of them, seeing Landru's picture in the newspapers, saved them this work and came forward voluntarily. Many more, however, were never traced. There was nothing left at Vernouillet to incriminate Landru and, at Gambais, most of the bodies had turned to dust. It was an almost impossible task. But piece by piece, little by little, the police built up a conclusive case. After two years of steady work, the trial finally came to court.

In the ancient courtroom of Versailles Henri Désiré Landru stood accused of the murder of ten women and of Mme Cuchet's son. Landru scowled at some of the witnesses, sneered icily at others and, at one, threw back his head and laughed. But the case against him was irrefutable. It was to be the guillotine for Henri Landru.

48

THE POISONED LANDLORD

He was a Frenchman who could speak no English, she an Englishwoman who spoke no French. On the sands of Biarritz they communicated their thoughts with a dictionary. It was a bizarre sight, and yet clearly the couple were in love.

Mabel Theresa Jones had met the forty-five-year-old Frenchman while he was staying at the Victoria Hotel. She had made no secret of her marriage. When Jean-Pierre Vaquier had asked about the ring on her finger she had told him all about her husband, Alfred, who ran the Blue Anchor Hotel in Byfleet, Surrey. She had also told him about her children. But Vaquier had not been put off.

It had begun as an innocent affair: a meal shared, a stroll on the beach, a peck on the cheek. Soon, however, it had developed into something far deeper. They spent the night together in Bordeaux. In Paris, too, a bed was shared. When it was time for her to return home, it was a tearful Mrs Jones who bade adieu. She doubted if she'd ever see her lover again.

On the very next day, however, Vaquier arrived in London. It was, ostensibly, a business trip. But he wasted little time in contacting his amour. As a result, Mabel Jones caught the next possible train to the capital.

She went to the hotel where Vaquier was staying, and he greeted her with typical enthusiasm and joy. He kissed her and took her to his bedroom. She stayed there for an hour before catching another train back to Byfleet. And she returned again the next day, this time staying overnight.

Fortune was evidently smiling on their illicit relationship because it was at this precise time that Mabel's 38-year-old husband was taken ill. He had caught a bad dose of 'flu in Margate and was confined to his bed. Jean-Pierre and Mabel made good use of his illness. Vaquier even moved down to take rooms at her husband's hotel and, in the days that followed many silent kisses and furtive glances were exchanged between the two.

But influenza doesn't last for ever and, soon enough, Arthur was up and about and attending to his chores. For Mabel this had drastic consequence. With a husband hovering in the background, her passion for Vaquier rapidly dimmed. Romance gave way to embarrassment and embarrassment to fear. Before long, she was imploring the Frenchman to leave.

Vaquier, however, was deaf to her entreaties. He continued to lodge at the Blue Anchor Hotel and positively refused to depart. February became March and still he wouldn't go. Slowly but surely, Mabel Jones was becoming desperate. By now she regretted ever having met the man.

Now Mr Jones was a heavy drinker. He would drink with any customer who visited his hotel and, on many occasions he drank far more than was good for him. After these drinking bouts he was in the habit, when he awoke in the morning, of taking a dose of salts which were kept in a bottle on the mantelpiece in the bar. Everyone in the hotel knew about this. Vaquier, who was invariably an early riser, could not fail to have noticed it.

On March 28th, 1924 there was something of a party at the hotel, and a good deal of liquor was consumed. Mr Jones as usual drank more than his fair share. He was, in fact, the last to go to bed.

The following morning he came downstairs. Still in his pyjamas, he went into the bar and went across for his dose of salts.

Immediately he had drunk from his glass he cried, "Oh God, it is bitter!"

Mrs Jones went across to him, took the glass, and poured the remains on to her hand. Cautiously, she tasted it with her tongue. She had to agree with her husband. There was clearly something wrong with it. Taking him by the hand, she led Alfred into the kitchen, got a glass of hot water and put some table salt into it. She gave this to her husband and commanded him to drink. He swallowed the mixture and, as a consequence, was violently sick. Mrs Jones thus reasoned that, if there had been anything wrong with his health salts, they were now safely out of his system.

But soon it was obvious that Alfred Jones was extremely ill. He was carried to his bedroom and his wife sent for a doctor. The licensee was in convulsions when the doctor arrived and, within a few minutes, he was dead. A fearful thought went through Mrs Jones's mind.

"You did it!" she declared, the moment she saw Vaquier.

The Frenchman went down on his knees, and took her hand. "Do you accuse me?" he asked.

"Yes," she replied curtly then, seizing a photograph of Vaquier which she had taken at Biarritz, she threw it on to the fire.

In due course it was established that Mr Jones had, indeed been murdered. Traces of strychnine were found in his stomach and intestines, and also in the glass which had contained his health salts. The police were called in.

It was at this point, according to Mabel Jones, that Vaquier made his confession. "Yes," he had told her, "I did it for you."

Vaquier would later deny this statement, but it made no difference. Already the police were building up other evidence against him. He had been seen in the bar before the tragedy occurred, he knew where the bottle was and, moreover, he had been seen handling the bottle on the mantelpiece after Jones had drunk from it.

Most damning of all was the evidence of a London chemist. Mr Horace Bland of Jones & Co. in Southampton

Row had a record of a man buying 12 grammes of strychnine just a few days before Jones's death. He had signed the poison book as J. Wanker, but, at an identification parade, it was J. Vaquier who the chemist picked out.

On July 2nd, 1924 Jean-Pierre Vaquier appeared at the Surrey Assizes in Guildford on the charge of murder.

In a loud clear voice he pleaded his innocence with the words "non coupable." He refuted the prosecutions assertion that he was "infatuated with the dead man's wife" and claimed he had no passion for Mrs Jones "except friendship as for a sister." "I assure you on the tomb of my mother that I am innocent," he declared.

The jury failed to believe him and, on Saturday, July 5th, they returned a verdict of guilty. The judge assumed the black cap and pronounced sentence of death.

Vaquier's case captured the public imagination, many of whom regarded him as an unfortunate victim in a tragedy of love. More than forty thousand people signed a petition calling for his reprieve, but it did no good. On August 12th, 1924, he was hanged at Wandsworth prison. He had paid the penalty for a fatal fascination of another man's wife.

As the noose was placed around his neck, he uttered his last words: "Vive la France!"

49

THE PERFECT MURDER

On the night of November 4th, 1938, Elisa Rebolledo was shot dead in the bedroom of her home in Bogota, Colombia. The money that she kept in her handbag was taken. The wall safe had been stripped clean.

Curiously, however, the valuable ring on the victim's finger had not been taken. Nor were there any signs of a struggle. Everything was neat and tidy and in its proper place. Moreover, though Elisa Rebolledo had been shot whilst standing, her body did not lie crumpled on the floor. Instead it had been carefully carried to her bed and laid out quite tenderly across it. So tranquil did it seem that, when the police first entered her room they thought the woman was sleeping. Only the bullet hole, just above her heart, made them think differently.

Chief Investigator Leonidas Ruilova was puzzled by the case. The most obvious suspect was Elisa's husband, Vicente. He had been pleading for a divorce so that he could marry his new love, so he probably wanted her out of the way. But Elisa had consented to a divorce only a few days previously. He no longer had any motive. Moreover, he lived more than one thousand miles away, in the coastal city of Barranquilla.

Dr Armando Gomez, a young attorney and the new man in Elisa's life was another possible suspect. Yet he too could be ruled out. Gomez had visited Elisa Rebolledo earlier in the evening, but he had been back home and in his apartment for some time at the time of her death.

That left just Rosa, Elisa's maid. She seemed an improbable killer but, when it was also established that her boyfriend was in the Rebolledo home on the night of the 4th, she quickly became the prime suspect. Rosa was collected from her sister's home and brought in for questioning. Of her boyfriend, however, there was no sign.

Whilst efforts were made to search him out, Ruilova caught a flight to Barranquilla. The quickest way to trace the jewellery, he reasoned, would be to get detailed descriptions of it from the husband. Rebolledo might also be able to tell him if there was anyone else who might have wanted this wife dead.

From the airport Ruilova took a cab to the hotel where Rebolledo lived.

Elisa's husband was no there. The hotel clerk told the chief that Rebolledo had got into a fight in a cafe and had spent the past few days in jail.

Ruilova found it easy to get information out of the talkative clerk. Rebolledo, it appeared, was a popular member of the younger crowd in the city and was making a success of his brokerage business. His fiancée, Piedad Ricaurte, was from one of the Barranquilla's wealthiest families.

The chief next drove to the jail where he was informed that Rebolledo had been released earlier that evening. The guard furnished Ruilova with the telephone number of Vicante's fiancée, he called the house. A servant told him that the young couple had gone to a hotel on the Puerto Colombia road, a few miles out of town. Twenty minutes of travelling over a rough dirt road brought Ruilova to a huge building with spreading lawns.

A waiter directed him to the couple, and the policeman asked quietly: "Are you Vicente Rebolledo?"

Both turned towards him in surprise and the man rose to his feet.

"Yes, that's right. Who are you?"

"Assistant Chief of the Bogota police." answered Ruilova. "I have flown here tonight to ask you a few questions regarding your estranged wife."

Rebolledo stared in bewilderment and said: "I'm afraid I don't understand."

"You were contemplating divorce," said the chief. "Is that correct?"

"Yes," answered the debonair young man, "but I can't see how that would interest the police."

"I understand that you had given her valuable jewellery at various times. Could you give me a good description of the pieces?"

"Certainly." A note of alarm entered the man's voice as he asked quickly: "Is anything wrong?"

"Yes," the chief answered, "Your wife was murdered last night."

Ruilova watched the husband's facial experession. The girl gave a startled gasp and clutched her companion. Rebolledo appeared dazed. He looked at the officer and said: "It doesn't seem possible. I had a letter from her only a day or so ago."

Rebolledo paused for a moment, then asked, "How did it happen? Who would have wanted to kill her? She had no enemies."

"We don't know the answers to your questions yet," the chief told him, "But we will find out soon enough, To do so, however, we need a description of her jewellery which was stolen."

"Then it must have been someone who knew the combination to the safe," commented Rebolledo.

"Yes, it seems so. Have you any suggestion as to who might have done it?" asked Ruilova.

The young man shook his head. "It doesn't seem real," he said.

Rebolledo did his best to describe the gems. Though Elisa wore them with no consideration to their worth, they were obviously very valuable pieces.

"Someone may had seen her wearing them and followed

her home to rob her," Rebolledo suggested.

"It's possible," Ruilova agreed. "Do you know Gomez, to whom she was engaged?"

"No, not personally, but I understand he is a man of exceptional character."

"What about the maid, Rosa?"

"She's been with Elisa a long time and, as far as I know, is completely trustworthy."

He went on to state that the only persons to benefit financial by Elisa's death were her relatives, who would inherit her estate.

Ruilova left the young man and returned to the hotel where he had taken a room. He telephoned a description of the missing jewellery to his assistants in Bogota and then began pacing up and down the room. He was puzzled by the day's events. Some things just didn't fit.

First thing next morning, Ruilova drove to the Barranquilla airport to make inquiries as to the passengers from Bogota during the past few days. As this was the nearest seaport, he thought the murderer might try to leave the country at this point with the victim's jewellery. He also got the local police to visit the city's pawnshops.

It was 4 o'clock in the afternoon when Leonidas Ruilova drove, once more, to Rebolledo's hotel.

"I think I've located one of the rings - the large ruby of which you spoke," he announced and, taking the ring from a leather pouch, he handed it over.

Rebolledo examined it long and hard. Tears began to form in his eyes, "It's like looking at a ghost," he whispered, "It brings back memories."

"I imagine it does," agreed the officer. "Memories of the night when you shot and killed your wife; then escaped with her jewellery and returned to Barranquilla by the early morning plane."

Rebolledo stared open-mouthed. "What is all this nonsense?" he declared, "You know I was in jail on the night Elisa was killed."

"It was that fact which gave me my first hint," the chief

announced "When I met you, I realised you were not the kind of man to be involved in café brawls. I learned you were an industrious and ambitious person who rarely drank, and that you had never before behaved in a wild fashion. Your alibi struck me as being too perfect. You had gone to too much trouble to establish it."

The accused man started to speak, but the chief stopped him.

"You see, at the airport I discovered that a certain "doctor" had travelled to Bogota on the afternoon of the murder, and returned the next morning. That man was using a passport number from a series not yet released, so he must have bribed a clerk in the department to issue him with it."

"I have not yet located the clerk, but the jail guard has confessed that you paid him 500 pesos to allow you to leave the jail for two days and falsify the records to make it appear that you had been there the entire four days. He has been arrested."

Rebolledo made protest of his innocence. But once the remainder of his wife's stolen jewellery was brought from his home, he confessed to it all.

"But why? What was your motive?" Ruilova demanded.

Rebolledo's answer was almost inaudible. "Because I could not bear to think of her as another man's wife. I did not know until recently that she was planning to remarry. I believed that she would never have anything to do with any man but me. I fell in love with her all over again and came here to plead with her to come back to me and not marry Gomez. She refused, so I shot her. I took her jewellery merely to make it look like robbery."

Ruilova stared at him incredulously.

"Do you mean to say that you cold-bloodedly killed your wife because you could not bear to think of her as another man's wife, even though you had deserted her for another woman?"

"Yes," replied the prisoner, "I am at peace now that she is dead and cannot marry Gomez."

In April 1939, Vicente Rebolledo was duly tried and convicted of his wife's murder. He was sentenced to 20 years in the penitentiary.

Incidentally the prison guard who had falsified the Rebolledo's records was also sent to prison and the clerk who had issued Rebolledo with false identification papers was reprimanded and dismissed from his job.

50

THE DEADLY DIVORCEE

Lady Pamela Wakefield was terrified lest news of the scandal should break in America, more terrified still after she had got her claws into the man of her dreams. Moses Worms was vastly wealthy, owning department stores in New Orleans, Chicago, Kansas City and New York and if he heard of Lady Pamela's divorce and adultery, she feared he would leave her without a second thought.

But, as the wedding grew nearer, Pamela grew more confident. He seemed blissfully unaware of her past, except those carefully censored extracts that she had told him. Everything was going perfectly. But then, just three days before the happy occasion, Moses's sister, Mrs Jennie Brock, dropped her bombshell.

"I've heard so much about you, my dear," she said in an ice-cold voice, "You must miss London very much. I don't know what I'd do if I didn't receive my English paper. I get all my news that way."

"We know everything about you," she added caustically, "We didn't learn in time to stop the wedding but I assure you we'll be keeping our eyes open."

Lady Pamela's jaw dropped. Moses had always spoken of his sister with a good deal of affection and she was certain that he would believe anything she'd say. She had no idea if Jennie had told him already, and there wasn't a moment during the next three days when she didn't expect to see him storm into the room, his sister's English newspaper in his hand, and denounce her as a strumpet.

But he didn't. The marriage went off exactly as planned. Lady Pamela Lee Wakefield became plain Pamela Worms and, to her husband, even plainer Pam, and they were ready for a blissful future.

Even so, Pamela knew that life would be intolerable with Jennie Brock close by and soon after the wedding she seated herself on her husband's knee, draped one arm around his neck and implored him to move house. "I think I'd like to see something else in America besides New Orleans," she said. "Since you have a store in Chicago, wouldn't it be possible to live there at least for a while?"

"That's a wonderful idea," declared Moses. "I've been thinking about some kind of change for us and that sounds perfect. I'll look into it first thing in the morning."

Pamela kissed him warmly and rubbed the back of his neck with her hand. Once away from the watchful eye of Jennie Brook, she was certain she could get to work on her master plan. Not for a moment had she wavered from her aim of mixing with the cream of London society and, with Moses's money it would be easily done. Pamela knew enough about society to realise that people would happily forgive the past indiscretions if you have a million or two in the bank.

That autumn, Moses, his bride and the two children from his first marriage, moved to Chicago. He also took along Annie, his elderly housekeeper who had been in his employ for many years. Pamela had not wanted her to join them. Despite Annie's advanced years, the woman managed to see and hear everything that went on in the household. Pamela also sensed that Annie disliked her, she suspected that she might even be a spy for Jennie Brock. However, since Moses insisted on keeping her, Pamela reluctantly agreed.

They found a large, comfortable estate on Lake Michigan and Pamela became mistress of a sizeable household with several servants. She was determined to get along with the children and succeeded in doing so admirably. She enchanted them with stories of the castle in which she had spent her childhood and engaged them in numerous different activities. Little Susan and her younger brother John were quickly besotted by her. A few weeks after they had settled down in Chicago, Moses announced that he would have to go to New York to check on one of his stores. He would be gone for several weeks.

As soon as he had left, Pamela decided to get a tight rein on the household, She was mortally afraid of any contact Moses might have with his sister or anyone else who could expose her secret. As it was, old Annie had the run of the household, and although Pamela had kept a careful lookout for any mail coming from New Orleans, she couldn't be sure that Annie didn't get to it first. So, she decided to hire a butler, someone who she could trust, someone who could keep an eye on the mail and on Annie at the same time. Her advertisement in the local paper ran: "Butler, young, handsome and discreet...."

Pamela interviewed some 30 applicants before finding the man who possessed all these qualifications. He was Hugo Wolfe, 32 years old, tall and athletic looking. "Every morning you are to collect the mail and bring it to me," Pamela said. "No one else but you is to handle it. I want you to be especially cautious about any mail postmarked New Orleans. Is that perfectly clear?"

For the next few months, Pamela managed to keep things on an even keel. She spent a good deal of time sorting out the mail, and from the letters Jennie Brock wrote to her brother, she knew she had taken the right step. In one letter there was an extremely well-informed account of the scandal in London. Another, which inquired why Moses hadn't answered her letters, enclosed a revealing clipping from a London newspaper. Jennie's mail arrived in a steady stream. Once she wrote: "If you don't have time to write a letter, Moses, at least drop me a line confirming you have received my letters. I'm beginning to think you are not receiving them at all." Pamela invariably read them through and then carefully burned them in the grate of her bedroom fireplace.

Moses Worms returned from New York briefly, but was compelled to be away from home for long spells to attend to his business. Whilst he was absent Pamela amused herself with her new butler, who was now also attending to more intimate duties for his mistress. But, whenever her husband returned, she would always be careful and attentive.

In August 1846, Moses Worms arrived home, weary after his journey from New York, where he had spent the past six months. After greeting her and the children warmly and distributing presents, he disappeared into the drawing room where he began to sort through the mail that had accumulated in his absence. A little later he emerged. His face was serious.

"I don't understand why I haven't received one letter from my family," he muttered. "It isn't like them. Especially Jennie."

Pamela said nothing.

Later, at dinner, he brought the subject up again: "I think I'm going to have to go down to New Orleans to see if everything is all right."

Pamela felt a sudden surge of panic. "No, don't," she said. "Please don't."

Moses looked surprised. Pamela was furiously searching her mind for a reason why he shouldn't go. But her thoughts were too full of the truth to come up with a really good lie. "I'm afraid if you go, you won't come back."

"What? Why do you talk like that?"

Pamela put her napkin to her eyes, which were perfectly dry. "I'm afraid they don't like me very much, Moses. I feel sure that's why they haven't written to you. They're disappointed with you for marrying me."

"Nonsense."

"I could tell, Moses. They wouldn't let on to you, but I could see it and feel it."

The idea was preposterous to Moses. As far as he was concerned, he had made a most fortunate marriage. Wasn't she a beautiful and cultivated woman? Who could possibly dislike her?

"I think you're making a mistake," he told her.

"It's no mistake on my part, dearest."

Moses was silent for a moment, then he jumped to his feet. "Well, if you're so certain about it, I'm going to New Orleans by the next coach. I'm going to set them straight!"

Pamela watched with increasing alarm as Moses summoned the servants, ordered them to pack his bags and to book a passage on the next coach to Memphis, where he would take the river steamer for New Orleans.

Pamela tried, but could find no good argument to keep him from going. She pulled out all the stops; tears, imploring, and protestations of love. Nothing worked. Moses Worms had made up his mind.

Next morning the carriage rolled away from the house in a cloud of dust, and Pamela went into the garden to sit and think.

A few hours later, little John Worms was stricken with a violent attack of stomach cramps. He was put to bed and a doctor was summoned. Pamela looked at the boy's pinched face, his little hands clutching his middle, and thought about how much her husband loved the boy. "We must notify Mr Worms at once," she told Wolfe. "Send a rider on horseback and try to overtake the coach before he boards the steamer at Memphis."

Two days later, Moses Worms was at the boy's bedside. The cramps continued. The doctor consulted and prescribed but nothing seemed to lessen the boy's suffering. At the end of three more days, he was dead. Moses was beside himself with grief.

Tears streamed down Pamela's cheeks as she tried to comfort him. She sought a little comfort, too. "Please, Moses," she said, "If you love me, don't leave me now."

"I wouldn't dream of it, Pam," he said hoarsely.

True to his word, Moses remained with Pamela until the New Year. Then he got an urgent message from New York and told Pamela that he would be away for several months.

In New Orleans, meanwhile, Jennie Brock was beside herself with worry. Moses had written to her, but in his letters he constantly reproached her for not writing back to him. As she had written to him every single week without fail, she was convinced that Pamela was intercepting her letters.

On March 18th Jenny Brock arrived unannounced at the door of her brother's mansion in Chicago. Pamela, who had no inkling of her coming, came downstairs to find her in the sitting room. She stifled a gasp, recovered, and managed a broad smile, welcoming her sister-in-law to the home.

Jennie did not return the smile. "You did not expect me, my dear, and you have little reason to welcome me. Where is my brother?"

"Oh dear me," said Pamela. "What a pity you didn't let me know that you were coming. Moses left for Europe three weeks ago."

As soon as the words had left her mouth, she realised that any servants especially Annie could easily expose the lie. This time she knew she had her work cut out.

She ordered that a bedroom be made up for Mrs Brock. "You must be very tired," she said, ignoring Jennie's less than friendly manner. "Why don't you rest until dinnertime? I'll have some refreshment sent up to you." Mrs Brock accepted her suggestion and allowed her luggage to be carried up to a room on the second floor. Pamela, meanwhile, went to the kitchen and prepared some chicken sandwiches and a glass of grape juice and told one of the servants to take these up to her uninvited guest.

Three hours later, Mrs Brock called out that she needed a doctor urgently. She had a fever and terrible pains in her stomach. The doctor was called, and prescribing some pills, said he would return the following day. Pamela was all sympathy. She insisted on preparing the trays for the sickroom. Next day, Mrs Brock was a little worse. The doctor prescribed more pills and Pamela remained solicitous. In her weakened condition, Jennie was actually grateful for these attentions. She even went so far as to apologise for all the trouble she was causing. On the third day, there were two doctors in attendance. They agreed that Mrs Brock was very weak and confided in Pamela that only a miracle could save her. Pamela, however, did not believe in miracles, and it seemed that her scepticism was vindicated when Jennie died in an agony of cramps and raging fever. When Pamela was quite certain her visitor was dead, she gently closed her eyes and pulled a sheet over her face and went downstairs to write to Moses.

It took several days for Moses to reach Chicago from New York, "How sad it is," Pamela told him, "that you missed seeing her. My worries that she didn't like me were groundless, Moses. We came to like each other a great deal."

During the next few weeks, Moses remained at home, but complained that the tragedies in their home made him feel depressed in the place. "I think I'd like to move somewhere else. How about Philadelphia?"

Pamela like the idea. In view of what she had in mind for her husband, it might be less suspicious if they lived somewhere new. Besides, it would provide an excellent excuse to engage some new servants. In particular, she wanted to get rid of the butler, Hugo, who was becoming for too demanding in his attentions.

Wolfe, however, didn't take kindly to the suggestion. "I'm going where you're going, sweetheart," he told her one afternoon when Moses was out. "What's more, I'm going in style."

"Your not going anywhere," Pamela said icily.

"You forget that I know a lot about you. I know more than you think. Those drops you put in her food. Drops that kill people have a habit of sticking around in their body for a while."

Pamela was in a fix. But she was in no position to bargain. Hugo moved with them to the new home in Philadelphia. He also continued to enjoy her bed.

In the meantime Pamela was also contemplating her grand plan. She knew that her husband's will divided his estate equally between herself and his daughter. She therefore resolved to tip it more favourably in her own direction.

In November Susan Worms was afflicted with a high fever and severe stomach cramps; much the same symptoms, the doctors observed, as those of the illness that had taken the life of Jennie Brock. Little Susan lingered for a week. As her pain-racked frame grew thinner and thinner, Moses went nearly insane with grief. Pamela, however, was a tower of strength. Always carrying food trays to the girl and ensuring that she took her medicine. But the disease, undiagnosed by six eminent doctors, continued to take her strength. After seven days she was dead.

Several months now passed and then, one night, when Moses was in New York, Hugo crept into Pamela's bedroom. Three hours later, he left. But this time he was back in her bedroom only a few seconds later.

"She saw me leave," he whispered anxiously.

"Who did?" Pamela demanded.

"Annie."

Pamela was gripped by a surge of anger. "I wish that old bag of bones was dead. Go in and strangle her," she ordered.

Hugo saw that she was in deadly earnest. "I can't do that," he said.

"Well I can," Pamela cried. She jumped out of bed, pulled a robe around her and marched out of the room. Down the hall she stormed then up the back stairway to the narrow little room at the top end of the house where the unsuspecting Annie slept. Wolfe followed her. He couldn't believe that she would carry out her threat, but he was wrong. In horror, he watched her fling open the door and throw herself on the elderly woman's bed. There was a frightening croaking sound as Pamela's long white fingers found the woman's bony neck, and then there was silence, broken only by heavy breathing.

Wolfe was aghast. Suddenly all feelings of romance for his mistress vanished. It probably crossed his mind that she was perfectly capable of murdering him too.

"Now, carry her out to the field behind the house and bury her," she ordered.

"Not me," he said, genuinely frightened by her viciousness.

"Yes, you. Don't forget that you stood idly by and did nothing to prevent me from strangling her. That makes you an accomplice, my friend. And besides, you know they'd never believe you if you said I did it but they might just believe me if I accuse you."

The butler saw the cold logic of her argument and, picking up the frail old body, carried it down the back stairs to the field and helped Pamela to bury it.

When they returned to the house, Pamela hurried into her husband's office and emerged with a wad of money in her hand. "Here's $500. This is all you'll ever get from me. Leave this house just as you are and never come back."

It was an order but, to Wolfe, it was also a good bargain. He never wanted to see or hear from her again.

When Moses returned Pamela told him that Annie and the butler had both vanished on the same night with the $500. She thought it likely that they had stolen the money, split the proceeds and gone their separate ways. Her husband didn't have any better ideas and didn't dispute hers.

As any trusting husband might, Moses had innocently confided to his wife that he had a great fondness for fresh mushrooms. Pamela said nothing but decided some time later that it would be better to go record as saying that she didn't like mushrooms in any form. It was a handy precaution for when, on the night of October 15th, 1851, they sat down to dinner and was served a dish of mushrooms, neither her husband nor the servant who waited on them saw anything unusual in the fact that Moses ate the whole dish himself.

A few minutes later, the unfortunate man turned white as a sheet, complained that he felt ill and needed to be helped to his bed. Doctors were summoned, but there was nothing they could do for him. They asked Pamela what he had eaten for dinner, and she told them that the cook had prepared, among other things, a dish of mushrooms.

The doctor nodded sagely, saying it was just as he thought, He added that he would like to speak to the cook. She came in, and in the doctor's presence explained that the mushrooms were fresh from the market and were fine ones as far as she could tell. The doctor and the woman left the room.

At dawn. Moses passed away. Pamela wept. The servants wept too. All except the cook. Just as the doctor was leaving she approached him and said she had something important to tell him. At that moment, Pamela came into the room, halted in her tracks and then rapidly turned and walked away.

Pamela knew very well what the cook was telling the doctor. It was about the mushrooms. The cook had bought a box from the market. They were on the kitchen table and she had just been about to cut them up for frying when she hear a noise behind her. She turned a little, and out of the corner of her eye she had seen Mrs Worms with another basket. The doctor saw her employer take a few of the new mushrooms out of the basket and put them with those she was preparing for dinner.

The doctor listened and decided that he was no judge of such things. This was a matter for the sheriff and an autopsy to decide.

Meanwhile, Pamela had rushed to her room, where she had taken down a small suitcase from her closet and crammed it full of clothes and money. She then ran out to the stables, hitched up a small brown mare to her carriage, and quickly rode off to town. There she caught the first coach going west to Pittsburgh.

Pamela's flight wasn't discovered until the sheriff arrived. Experience told him that this sort of hasty departure was a sure sign of guilt, and he ordered her arrest.

Pamela was far too distinguished and beautiful to escape notice. She was quickly traced to Pittsburgh where it was learned that she had taken passage on a river steamer.

Pamela was found in her cabin. Her only effort to resist arrest was to faint.

By the time she was returned to Philadelphia under police guard, medical examiners had identified the poisonous variety of mushroom in Moses Worms' stomach. Confronted with this evidence and with that of the cook, Pamela decided to tell all. The story was much longer and more grisly than her captors had anticipated. She told them about her London scandal and about numerous other romantic escapades which would have caused just as much of a stir had they been discovered. She freely admitted the murder of Worms' two children and sister by laudanum and also to murdering Annie. The elderly servant's remains were removed from the makeshift grave behind the house. Moses Worms was, Pamela confessed, her fifth victim.

After making her confession, Pamela recanted. But by the time she came to trial she had changed her mind once more and decided to reveal all. Before a packed gallery, she related the story of her life, omitting none of the gory details.

It took the jury just five minutes to find her guilty. The court sentenced her to die on the gallows. She was hanged before a large crowd in Pittsburgh, Pennsylvania on January 30th, 1852.

INDEX OF VILLAINS